Junior Colour Knits

a colourful collection of hand knit designs for cool kids from 3 months to 5 years

erika knight
MADE IN ENGLAND

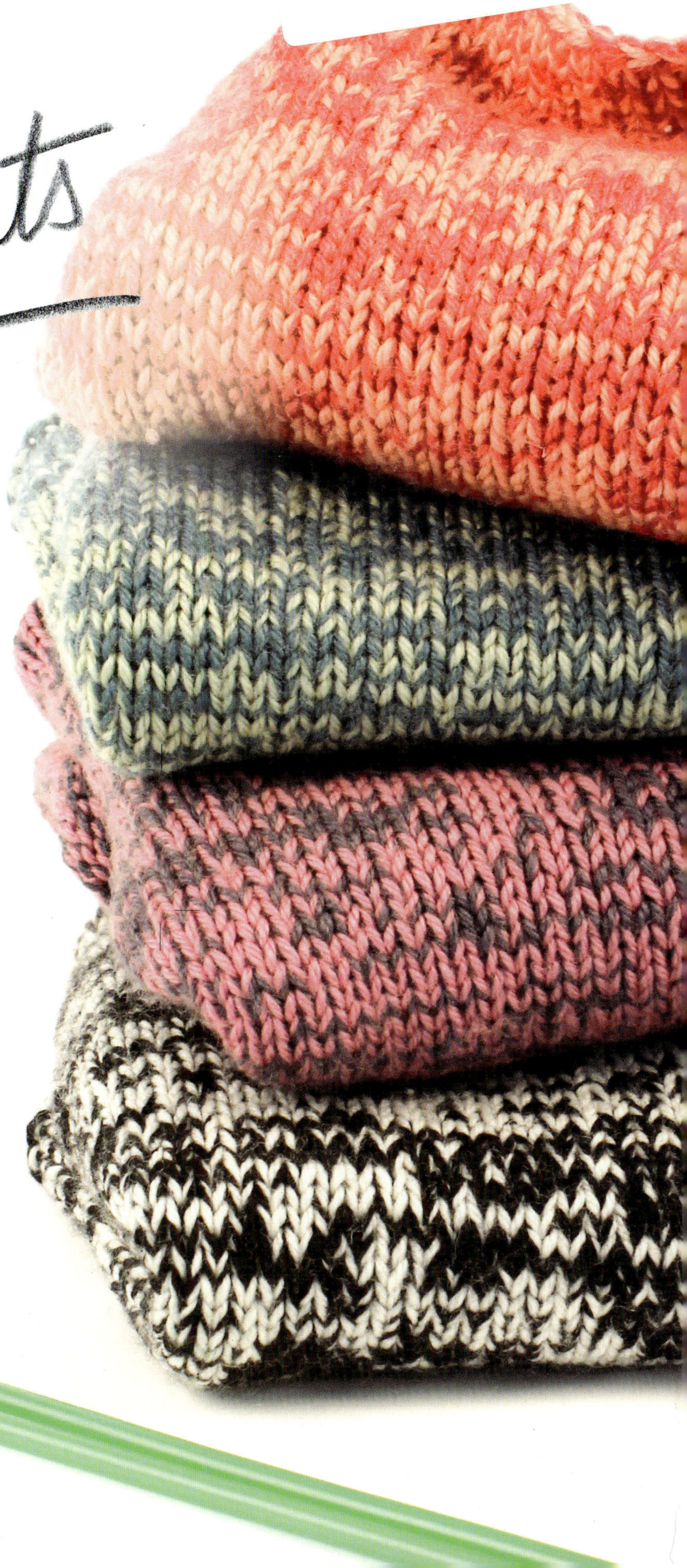

QUAIL
www.quailpublishing.co.uk

JUNIOR COLOUR KNITS

First published in Great Britain in 2015 by
Quail Publishing
www.quailpublishing.co.uk

Copyright © Quail Publishing 2015 & Erika Knight with Ramsden Ltd 2015.

All rights reserved. No part of this publication may be reproduced, stored in a retrieval system or transmitted in any form or by any means, electronic, electrostatic, magnetic tape, mechanical, photocopying, recording or otherwise without the prior permission in writing from the publishers. Designs may also not be made for resale.

Designs: Erika Knight
Pattern Checking: Sally Lee
Photography: Parents of the models & Quail Studio
Graphic Design: Quail Studio
Concept: Arabella Harris

ISBN 978-0-9927707-7-8

Printed in the United Kingdom

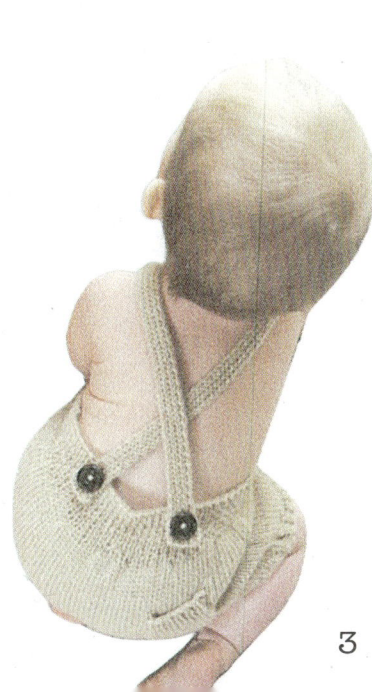

CONTENTS

5 YARNS

8 HOW TO MEASURE YOUR CHILD

13 SCRIBBLE JUMPER

17 PINAFORE DRESS

23 BOBBLY HAT

27 FUR VEST

31 COLOUR BLOCK JUMPER

37 BALACLAVA

41 TIPPED TANK TOP

47 FURRY PARKA

51 ROMPER

57 LEGGINGS

63 VARSITY CARDY

73 SCRAP BANDIT

78 BASIC INFO / ABBREVIATIONS

80 WORKSHOP

82 FINISHING

84 THANKS TO

Yarns

The yarns recommended in this book are all from the Erika Knight yarn collection and are all 100% natural wools made entirely in Britain from British sheep breeds - British Blue wool, Maxi wool and Fur wool. Wool is naturally soft, comfortable and sustainable.

British Blue Wool

Double knit
Pure British Bluefaced Leicester Wool – 100% wool
55m / 60yds – 25g ball
machine washable @ 30°C
3.75-4 mm / US 6-7 knitting needles

Fur Wool

mulberry   marni   manga   steve

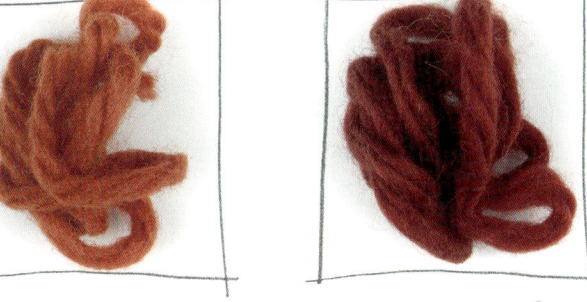

parker   mallard

Super chunky
Pure British Wool – 97% wool, 3% nylon binder
40m / 44yds – 100g hank
10-12mm / US 15-17 knitting needles

Maxi Wool

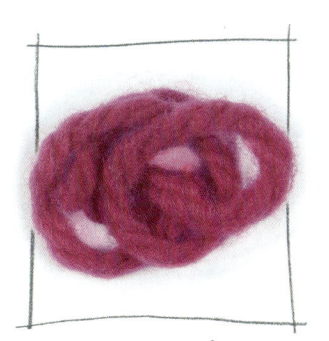

manga   marni   miss pinkaby   classic

mallard   steve   storm

Super chunky
Pure British Wool –
100% wool
80m / 87yds – 100g hank
10-12mm / US 15-17
knitting needles

How to measure your child

Knitting a cardigan?

HOW TO MEASURE

1. chest - measure around the fullest part of the chest, close under the arms

2. length - measure from centre of the back of the neck to the natural waistline, or from the top of the shoulder to the hem of your favourite sweater.

3. waist - measure around the natural waistline, usually just above the belly-button.

4. sleeve length - with arm slightly bent, measure from armpit to wrist

5. armhole length - with arm outstretched, measure from the top, outside edge of the shoulder, down to the armpit

6. head - measure from the centre forehead, around the head, keeping the tape measure snug

The projects in this book are designed to fit little children from approx. 3 months to 5 years of age comfortably .
The sizing guide on each pattern gives both a chest size and a length measurement for the garment. The amount of ease has been calculated for each individual design to create a particular look, which may vary from pattern to pattern. An approximate age is given in each pattern, but it is essential to measure your child (or a favourite sweater that fits the child well) and to choose the size to knit based on these measurements, and not only the age to ensure a good fit.

*of course if your child cannot stand up yet – measure baby laying down.

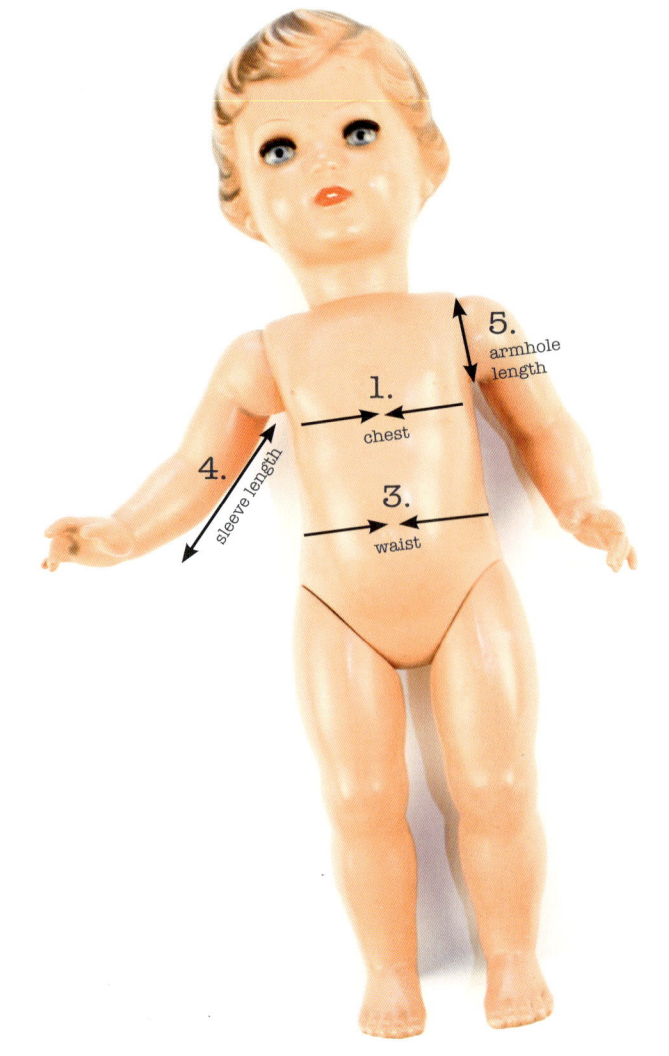

Another way to choose which size to knit is to measure a favourite sweater, which fits the child well.

NOTE
The most important measurement to start with is chest width. The body length of the garment, or the sleeve length, can be easily adjusted – for example you can add or subtract rows before you start the armhole shaping.

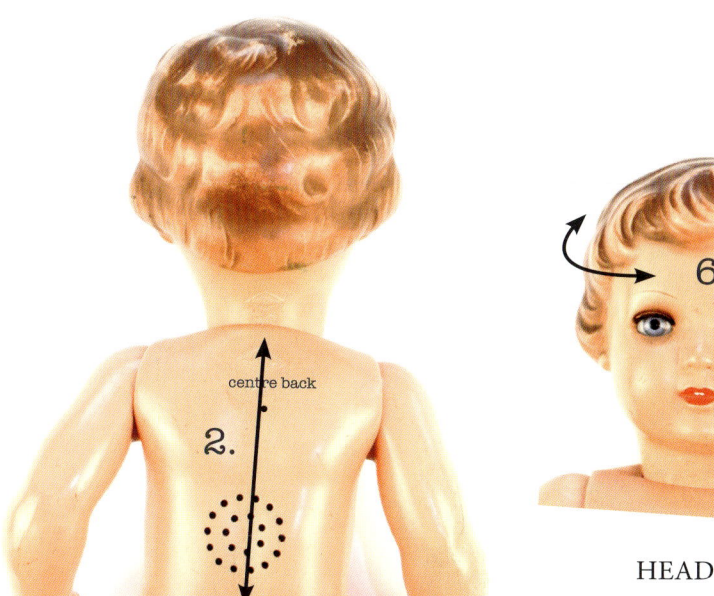

BACK

HEAD

Measurements look like this in the pattern.

MEASUREMENTS Approx. age	3-6mths	6-12mths	1-2yrs	2-3 yrs	4-5 yrs
To fit chest	43cm/17in	45.5cm/18in	50.5cm/20in	53cm/21in	58.5cm/23in
Finished size	54cm/21¼in	58cm/22¾in	62cm/24¼in	66cm/26in	70cm/27½in
Chest flat	27cm/10½in	29cm/11½in	31cm/12¼in	33cm/13in	35cm/13¾in
Length	27cm/10½in	30cm/11¾in	33cm/13in	36cm/14in	39cm/15in
Sleeve seam	17cm/6¾in	20cm/8in	23cm/9¼in	26cm/10½in	29cm/11½in

Projects

01. SCRIBBLE JUMPER

Easy peasy basic jumper knitted with two strands of wool as one yarn. Worked in stocking / stockinette stitch all the way so cuffs and hems will roll up to show further texture and with a cosy little funnel neck.

MATERIALS
erika knight British blue wool 100% Bluefaced Leicester wool, 55m/60yds – 25g ball
A 4(5:6:7:7) balls
B 4(5:6:7:7) balls
5mm / US 8 and 5.5mm / US 9 needles
large eyed blunt tipped sewing needle

MEASUREMENTS

Approx. age	3-6mths	6-12mths	1-2yrs	2-3 yrs	4-5 yrs
To fit chest	43cm /17in	45.5cm/18in	50.5cm/20in	53cm/21in	58.5cm/23in
Finished size	54cm/21¼in	58cm/22¾in	62cm/24¼in	66cm/26in	70cm/27½in
Chest flat	27cm/10½in	29cm/11½ in	31cm/12¼in	33cm/13in	35cm/13¾in
Length	27cm/10½in	30cm/11¾in	33cm/13in	36cm/14in	39cm/15in
Sleeve seam	17cm/6¾in	20cm/8in	23cm/9¼in	26cm/10½in	29cm/11½in

TENSION / GAUGE
15.5 sts and 22 rows to 10 cm / 4in meas over St st using 5.5 mm/US 9 needles. Change needle size, if necessary, to ensure the correct tension.

MAKE

BACK AND FRONT THE SAME
With 5mm / US 8 needles and A and B held together as one yarn cast on 42(45:48:52:56)sts.
Starting with a K row work in St st for 3cm / 1¼in
Change to 5.5mm / US 9 needles cont in St st until work meas 17(19:20:22:24)cm /6¾ (7½:8:8¾:9½)in, ending with RS facing for next row.

SHAPE ARMHOLES
Next row: Cast / bind off 2(2:2:3:3)sts at beg of next 2 rows. 38(41:42:46:50)sts
Cont straight until armhole meas 11(12:13:14:15)cm / 4¼ (4¾:5¼:5¾:6)in, ending with RS facing for next row.

SHAPE SHOULDERS
Cast / bind off 5(5:5:6:6)sts at beg of next 2 rows. 28(31:32:34:38)sts.
Work 4(4:4:6:6)rows straight.
Work funnel neck as foll on these sts:
Next row: K2, K2tog, K to last 4 sts, K2tog tbl, K2.
Next row: P.
Rep last 2 rows until 24(27:28:30:34)sts rem. Cast / bind off loosely.

SLEEVES (MAKE 2 THE SAME)

With 5mm / US 8 needle and A and B held together as one yarn, cast on 24(26:28:30:32)sts and starting with a K row work in St st for 3cm / 1¼in ending with RS facing for next row.

Change to 5.5mm/ US 9 needles and work 4(6:8:8:8)rows.

Next row (inc): K2, inc in next st, K to last 3 sts, inc in next st, K2.

Inc 1 st at both ends as above on every foll 6th row until 34(38:40:44:48)sts.

Cont straight until work meas 18.5(21.5:24.5:27.5:30.5)cm / 7¼ (8½:9¾:10¾:12)in from cast on edge, ending with RS facing for next row.

Cast / bind off loosely.

FINISH

Weave in any long ends. Gently steam work on reverse to enhance the yarn. Sew both shoulders and neck seams. Sew sleeves into armholes. Sew side and sleeve seams.

02. PINAFORE DRESS

02. PINAFORE DRESS

Simply styled pinafore dress, knitted in stocking / stockinette stitch with garter stitch hem and trims with integral fully fashion shaping to give a lovely fit and a little flare. Make it in solid colour or in a stripe pattern.

MATERIALS
erika knight British blue wool 100% Bluefaced Leicester wool, 55m/60yds – 25g ball
Solid colour
A 5(6:7:8:9) balls
5 colour stripe
A 4(4:5:6:7) balls
B 2(2:2:2:2) balls
C 2(2:2:2:2) balls
D 2(2:2:2:2) balls
E 2(2:2:2:2) balls
3.25mm/US 3 and 3.75mm/US 5 needles
Stitch holders
Large eyed blunt tipped sewing needle

MEASUREMENTS

Approx. age	3-6mths	6-12mths	1-2yrs	2-3 yrs	4-5 yrs
To fit chest	43cm/17in	45.5cm/18in	50.5cm/20in	53cm/21in	58.5cm/23in
Actual chest	48cm/19in	52cm/20½	58cm/22¾in	62cm/24½in	68cm/26¾
Chest flat	24cm/9½in	26cm/10¼in	29cm/11½in	31cm/12¼in	34cm/13½in
Length	35.5cm/14in	38.5cm/15 ¼in	41.5cm/16in	44cm/17½in	47cm/18½in
Armhole length	11.5cm/4½in	12.5cm/5in	13.5cm/5¼in	14cm/5½in	15cm/6in

TENSION / GAUGE
23 sts and 30 rows to 10 cm / 4in meas over St st using 3.75 mm/US 5 needles. Change needle size if necessary to ensure the correct tension.

NOTES
Striping or joining in a new ball- on row before you need the new colour, work to the last stitch.
Taking the end of the new colour, use together with the yarn in work to work the last stitch, creating a 'double stitch'
On the first stitch of next row, work the double stitch as one stitch with just the end of the new colour. This will securely 'anchor' your new yarn and not create unsightly knots nor create bumps.

5 COLOUR STRIPE SEQUENCE

*A   2 rows
B   2 rows
A   2 rows
C   2 rows
A   2 rows
D   2 rows
A   2 rows
E   2 rows
repeat from *

MAKE

BACK AND FRONT THE SAME

Using 3.25mm/US 3 needles and A cast on 75(81:87:93:99) sts and work 4 rows in g st.

Following the stripe sequence as above and changing in colours as per note, work as folls:

Change to 3.75mm/US 5 needles and starting with a K row work 8(10:12:12:14) rows in St st.

Next row (dec): K12(14:16:18:20), K2tog, K1, K2tog tbl, K41(43:45:47:49), K2tog, K1, K2tog tbl, K12(14:16:18:20). 71(77:83:89:95) sts

Work 11(11:13:15:15) rows straight.

Next row (dec): K11(13:15:17:19), K2tog, K1, K2tog tbl, K39(41:43:45:47), K2tog, K1, K2tog tbl, K11(13:15:17:19). 67(73:79:85:91)sts

Work 11(11:13:15:15) rows straight.

Next row (dec): K10(12:14:16:18), K2tog, K1, K2tog tbl, K37(39:41:43:45), K2tog, K1, K2tog tbl, K10(12:14:16:18). 63(69:75:81:87) sts

Work 11(11:13:15:15) rows straight.

Next row (dec): K9 (11:13:15:17), K2tog, K1, K2tog tbl, K35(37:39:41:43), K2tog, K1, K2tog tbl, K9(11:13:15:17). 59(65:71:77:83) sts

Work 11(11:13:15:15) rows straight.

Next row (dec): K8(10:12:14:16), K2tog, K1, K2tog tbl, K33(35:37:39:41), K2tog, K1, K2tog tbl, K8(10:12:14:16). 55(61:67:73:79)sts

Cont straight until work meas 24(26:28:30:32) cm / 9½ (10¼:11:11¾:12½)in from cast on edge, ending with RS facing for next row.

SHAPE ARMHOLES

Cast / bind off 3(3:4:4:4) sts at beg of next 2 rows. 49(55:59:65:71) sts

Next row: K3, K2tog, K to last 5 sts, K2tog tbl, K3.

Next row: P3, P2tog tbl, P to last 5 sts, P2tog, P3.

Dec as set above at both ends of every row until 41(43:45:49:53) sts rem.

Cont straight until armhole meas 5(5.5:5.5:6.5:7) cm / 2(2¼:2¼:2½:2¾)in, ending with RS facing for next row.

SHAPE NECK

K15(15:16:17:19), **TURN** and leave rem sts on a holder

Next row: P

Next row: K to last 5 sts, K2tog tbl, K3.

Next row: P

Rep last 2 rows until 8(8:9:10:10) sts rem

Cont straight until armhole meas 11.5(12.5:13.5:14:15)cm / 4½(5:5¼:5½:6¾)in, ending with RS facing for next row. Leave sts on a holder.

Place centre 11(13:13:15:15) sts on a holder.

With RS of work facing, re-join yarn to rem sts and K to the end of row.

Next row: P

Next row: K3, K2tog, K to end.

Next row: P

Rep last 2 rows until 8(8:9:10:10) sts rem.

Cont straight until armhole meas 11.5(12.5:13.5:14:15)cm / 4½ (5:5¼:5½:6¾)in, ending with RS facing for next row. Leave sts on a holder.

Graft one shoulder using three-needle method, with WS of work facing to make a ridge on the RS. (see workshop page 80-81)

NECKBAND
With A and RS of work facing and 3.25mm/ US 3 needles, pick up and K16(17:18:18:19) sts down side of neck, 11(13:13:15:15) sts from holder, 16(17:18:18:19) sts up side of neck to the shoulder, 16(17:18:18:19) sts down side of neck, 11(13:13:15:15)sts from holder and 16(17:18:18:19)sts up side of neck. 86(94:98:102:106) sts.
Work 4 rows g st.
Cast/ bind off.

Graft the second shoulder using the three-needle method and join the neckband seam.

ARMBANDS
With A and RS of work facing and 3.25mm/US 3 needles pick up and K 54(60:66:72:78)sts around each armhole and work 4 rows g st.
Cast / bind off.

FINISH
Weave in any long ends. Gently steam work on reverse to enhance the yarn. Join side seams.

03. BOBBLY HAT

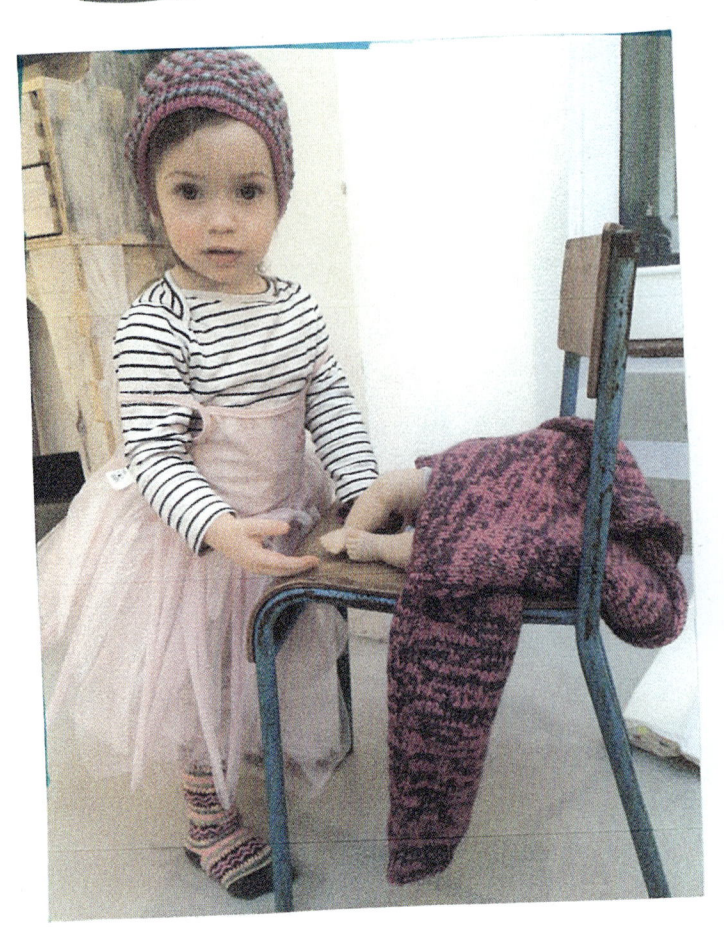

03. BOBBLY HAT

An all time favourite texture stitch with really easy shaping to create a cosy retro style beanie hat. This one is worked in three colours, but why not use up scraps from other projects for a multi-colour hat.

MATERIALS

erika knight British blue wool 100% Bluefaced Leicester wool 55m/60yds - 25g ball
A - 1 (1) ball
B - 1 (1) ball
C - 1 (1) ball
3.75mm/US 5 and 4mm/US 6 needles
large eyed blunt tipped sewing needle

MEASUREMENTS

Approx. age	3-12mths	2-5years
Head circumference	35.5cm/14in	40.5cm/16in
Finished length	19cm /7½in	21cm/8¼in

TENSION / GAUGE

23 sts and 30 rows to 10cm / 4in meas over St st using 3.75mm / US 5 needles. Change needle size if necessary to ensure the correct tension.

STRIPE SEQUENCE

2 rows A
2 rows B
2 rows C

MAKE

Using 3.75mm/US 5 needles and A cast on 102 (110)sts and foll the stripe sequence above work 10(12) rows in K1, P1 rib. Change to 4mm/US 6 needles and keeping stripe sequence correct work in bobbly st as foll:

Row 1 (WS): K1, *(K1, P1, K1) into next st, P3tog; rep from * to last st, K1.
Row 2 (RS): P.
Row 3: K1,*P3tog, (K1, P1, K1) into next st; rep from * to last st, K1.
Row 4: P.
Rep last 4 rows until work meas 16.5(18.5)cm/ 6½ (7¼)in from the cast on edge, finishing at the end of **row 1**, with RS facing for next row.

SHAPE TOP

Next row: (P1, P3tog) to last 2 sts, P2. 52(56) sts
Next row: K.
Next row: (P1, P3tog) to end. 26(28) sts
Next row: K.
Next row (1st size only): (P1, P3tog) to last 2 sts, P2. 14 sts.
Next row (2nd size only): (P1, P3tog) to end of row. 14 sts.

FINISH

Cut yarn leaving a long end, thread through rem sts, pull up tightly and secure, gently steam on reverse, then join the seam.

04. FUR VEST

A simple vest knitted in garter stitch with big needles and made in natural fur wool. A quick and easy piece to make, and a great piece to layer over Tees and sweats.

MATERIALS
erika knight fur wool 97% British wool, 3% nylon binder, 40m/44yds -100g/3½ oz hank
2(2:2:3) hanks
10mm /US 15 needles
large eyed blunt tipped sewing needle

MEASUREMENTS

Approx. age	6-12mths	1-2yrs	2-3yrs	4-5yrs
Finished size	50cm/20in	56cm/22in	60cm/23¾in	64cm/25¼in
Length	26cm/10¼in	29cm/11½in	32cm/12¾in	34cm/13½in
Armhole length	11cm/4½in	12cm/4¾in	13cm/5¼in	14cm/5½in

TENSION/ GAUGE
7 sts and 11 rows to 10 cm / 4in meas over g st using 10 mm/US 15 needles. Change needle size, if necessary, to ensure the correct tension.

MAKE

BACK
Cast on 20(22:24:26) sts and work 7(8:9:10) cm / 2¾ (3¼:3½:4)in in g st.
Dec 1 st at both ends of next row. 18(20:22:24) sts.
Work straight until back meas 12(14:17:19) cm / 4¾ (5½:6¾:7½)in from cast on edge. Place a marker at both ends of last row to show start of armhole shaping.

SHAPE ARMHOLES
Cast / bind off 1 st at beg of next 2 rows. 16(18:20:22) sts.
Dec 1 st at both ends of next row. 14(16:18:20) sts.
Cont straight until armhole meas 11(12:13:14) cm / 4¼ (4¾:5¼:5½) in from marker.

SHAPE SHOULDERS AND BACK NECK
Next row: K4 (5:5:6), **TURN**.
Cast / bind off rem 4(5:5:6) sts.
Rejoin yarn to rem sts.
Cast / bind off centre 6(6:8:8) sts, K to end of row. 4(5:5:6) sts.
Next row: K.
Cast / bind off rem 4(5:5:6) sts.

FRONTS - MAKE 2 ALIKE
Cast on 7(8:9:10) sts and work in g st as folls:
Next row: K
Next row: Inc 1 st at beg of row. 8(9:10; 11) sts
Next row: Inc 1 st at end of row. 9(10:11:12) sts.
Next row: Inc 1 st at beg of row. 10(11:12; 13) sts.
Cont straight until front meas 7(8:9:10) cm 2¾ (3¼:3½:4) in from cast on edge, ending at side seam (the straight edge, not the shaped edge).
Dec 1 st at beg of next row. 9(10:11:12) sts.
Work straight until front meas

12(14:17:19) cm 4¾(5½:6¾:7½) in from cast on edge, ending at side seam. Place marker to show start of armhole shaping.

SHAPE ARMHOLE

Cast / bind off 1 st at beg of row, K to end. 8(9:10:11) sts.
Work 1 row straight.
Dec 1 st at beg of next row. 7(8:9:10) sts.
Cont straight until armhole meas 7(8:8:9) cm / 2¾ (3¼:3¼:3½)in from marker, ending at centre front.

SHAPE NECK

Dec 1 st at neck edge on next 3(3:4:4) rows. 4(5:5:6) sts.
Work straight until armhole matches back to shoulder shaping.
Cast / bind off rem 4(5:5:6) sts.

FINISH

Weave in any yarn ends. Lay pieces out flat and gently steam and pull into shape. Sew shoulder seams. Sew side seams matching cast on edges and armhole markers.

05. COLOUR BLOCK JUMPER

05. COLOUR BLOCK JUMPER

Simple repeating stitch patterns worked to create a classic Aran-style jumper, updated with bold blocks of colour.

MATERIALS

erika knight British blue wool 100% Bluefaced Leicester wool 55m/60yds - 25g ball
A - 3(3:4:4:5) balls
B - 1(1:1:1:1) balls
C - 5(5:6:6:7) balls
3.75mm/US 5 and 4mm/US 6 needles
stitch holders
cable needle
large eyed blunt tipped sewing needle

MEASUREMENTS

Approx. age	3-6mths	6-12 mths	1-2 yrs	2-3 yrs	4-5 yrs
To fit chest	43cm/17in	45.5cm/18in	50.5cm/20in	53cm/21in	58.5cm /23in
Finished size	54cm/21¼in	58cm/22¾in	62cm/241/4in	66cm/26in	70cm/27½in
Chest flat	27cm/10½in	29cm/11¼in	31cm/12¼in	33cm/13in	35cm/13¾in
Length	27cm/10¾in	31cm/12¼in	35cm/14in	39cm/15½in	43cm/17in
Sleeve seam	15cm/6in	18cm/7¼in	21cm/8½in	24cm/9½in	27cm/10¾in

TENSION / GAUGE

23 sts and 30 rows to 10cm / 4in meas over St st using 3.75mm/US 5 needles. Change needle size if necessary to ensure the correct tension.

NOTES

Changing colour or joining in a new ball- on row before you need the new colour, work to the last stitch.
Taking the end of the new colour, use together with the yarn in work to work the last stitch, creating a 'double stitch'
On the first stitch of next row, work the double stitch as one stitch with just the end of the new colour. This will securely 'anchor' your new yarn and not create unsightly knots nor create bumps.

SPECIAL ABBREVIATIONS

C4F – slip next 2 sts onto cable needle and hold at front of work knit next 2 sts from LH needle, then knit sts from cable needle.
C4B - slip next 2 sts onto cable needle and hold at back of work knit next 2 sts from LH needle, then knit sts from cable needle.
C6B - slip next 3 sts onto cable needle and hold at back of work knit next 3 sts from LH needle, then knit sts from cable needle.
C12F – slip next 6 sts onto cable needle and hold at front of work knit next 6 sts from LH needle, then knit sts from cable needle.
C12B - slip next 6 sts onto cable needle and hold at back of work knit next 6 sts from LH needle, then knit sts from cable needle.

CABLE RIB

Row 1 (RS): K3, *(P1, K1tbl) twice, P1, K3, rep from * to end.
Row 2: P3, *(K1, P1tbl) twice, K1, P3, rep from * to end.
Row 3: K3, *P1, sl next 2 sts onto cable needle and hold at front of work, K1tbl, then P1, K1tbl from cable needle, P1, K3, rep from * to end.
Row 4: P3, *(K1, P1tbl) twice, K1, P3, rep from * to end.
Row 5: K3, *(P1, K1tbl) twice, P1, K3, rep from * to end.
Row 6: P3, *(K1, P1tbl) twice, K1, P3, rep from * to end.
Rep these 6 rows.

MAKE

BACK

Using 3.75mm/US 5 needles and A cast on 75(83:91:99:107)sts and work 4(4:5:5:5) cm / 1½ (1½ :2:2:2) in, in cable rib, ending with RS facing for next row and dec 1 st on last row. 74(82:90:98:106)sts.

Change to 4mm/US 6 needles and cont in double moss st, cables and honeycomb centre panel patt as foll:

Row 1 (RS): (K1, P1) x 5(7:7:9:11)times, K2, P2, K6, P2, K1, P2, (C4B, C4F) x 3(3:4:4:4)times, P2, K1, P2, K6, P2, K2, (P1, K1) x 5(7:7:9:11) times.

Row 2: (P1, K1) x 5(7:7:9:11)times, P2, K2, P6, K2, P1, K2, P24(24:32:32:32), K2, P1, K2, P6, K2, P2, (K1, P1) x 5(7:7:9:11)times.

Row 3: (P1, K1) x 5(7:7:9:11)times, K2, P2, C6B, P2, K1, P2, K24(24:32:32:32), P2, K1, P2, C6B, P2, K2, (K1, P1) x 5(7:7:9:11)times.

Row 4: (K1, P1) x 5(7:7:9:11)times, P2, K2, P6, K2, P1, K2, P24(24:32:32:32), K2, P1, K2, P6, K2, P2, (P1, K1) x 5(7:7:9:11)times.

Row 5: (K1, P1) x 5(7:7:9:11)times, K2, P2, K6, P2, K1, P2, (C4F, C4B) x 3(3:4:4:4) times, P2, K1, P2, K6, P2, K2, (P1, K1) x 5(7:7:9:11)times.

Row 6: (P1, K1) x 5(7:7:9:11)times, P2, K2, P6, K2, P1, K2, P24(24:32:32:32), K2, P1, K2, P6, K2, P2, (K1, P1) x 5(7:7:9:11)times.

Row 7: (P1, K1) x 5(7:7:9:11)times, K2, P2, K6, P2, K1, P2, K24(24:32:32:32), P2, K1, P2, K6, P2, K2, (K1, P1) x 5(7:7:9:11)times.

Row 8: (K1, P1) x 5(7:7:9:11)times, P2, K2, P6, K2, P1, K2, P24(24:32:32:32), K2, P1, K2, P6, K2, P2, (P1, K1) x 5(7:7:9:11)times.

Rep these 8 rows until work meas 15(17:17:19:21)cm / 6(6¾ :6¾ :7½ : 8¼)in from cast on edge, ending with RS facing for next row.

Change to B and work 3(3:4:4:4)cm/ 1¼ (1¼ :1½ :1½ : 1½)in, ending with RS facing for next row.

SHAPE ARMHOLES

Change to C and cast / bind off 3(4:5:5:5) sts at beg of next 2 rows.
Dec 1 st at both ends of next 4(5:5:6:7) rows. 60(64:70:76:82)sts.
Keeping patt correct cont straight until armhole meas 10(11:12:13:14)cm/ 4(4¼:4¾:5¼:5½)in ending with RS facing for next row.

SHAPE SHOULDERS AND BACK NECK

Cast / bind off 7(7:8:9:10) sts at beg of next row.

Patt until 10(10:12:12:13)sts on RH needle, **TURN.**

Next row: Cast / bind off 2(2:3:3:3)sts, patt to end of row.

Next row: Cast / bind off rem 8(8:9:9:10)sts.

With RS of work facing slip centre 26(30:30:34:36)sts onto a holder. Rejoin C to rem sts and patt to end of row.

Cast / bind off 7(7:8:9:10) sts, patt to end of row.

Next row: Cast / bind off 2(2:3:3:3)sts, patt to end of row.

Cast / bind off rem 8(8:9:9:10)sts.

FRONT

Work as back until armhole meas 7(8:8:9:10)cm / 2¾ (3¼:3¼:3½:4)in, ending with RS facing for next row.

SHAPE NECK

Next row: Patt 20(20:22:25:27)sts, **TURN.**

Next row: Cast / bind off 3 sts at beg of row, patt to end.

Dec 1 st at neck edge on every row until 15(15:17:18:20)sts rem.

Work straight until armhole matches back to start of shoulder shaping, ending with RS facing for next row.

SHAPE SHOULDER

Cast / bind off 7(7:8: 9:10) sts.
Work 1 row.
Cast / bind off rem 8(8:9:9:10) sts.
With RS of work facing, slip centre 20(24:26:26:28)sts onto a holder.

Rejoin C to rem sts and patt to end of row.
Work 1 row straight.

Next row: Cast / bind off 3 sts at beg of row, patt to end.

Dec 1 st at neck edge on every row until 15(15:17:18:20)sts rem.

Work straight until armhole matches back to start of shoulder shaping, ending with WS facing for next row.

SHAPE SHOULDER

Cast / bind off 7(7:8: 9:10) sts.
Work 1 row.
Cast / bind off rem 8(8:9:9:10) sts.

GIANT BRAID PANEL WORKED OVER 18 STS

Row 1 (RS): K18.
Row 2: P18,
Row 3: K6, C12F.
Row 4: P18.
Rows 5 – 10: Rep row 1 and row 2, 3 times.
Row 11: C12B, K6.
Row 12: P18.
Rows 13 – 16: Rep row 1 and row 2, twice.
Rep these 16 rows.

SLEEVES

Using 3.75mm/US 5 needles and C, cast on 43(43:51:51:51) sts and work 4(4:5:5:5) cm/1½ (1½:2:2:2) in, in cable rib, ending with RS facing for next row and dec 1 st at end of last row. 42(32:50:50:50)sts.

Change to 4mm/US 6 needles and work in double moss st and giant braid as foll:

Row 1: (K1,P1) x 4(4:6:6:6)times, K2, P2, K18 (row 1 of giant braid cable), P2, K2, (P1, K1) x 4(4:6:6:6)times.

Row 2: (P1, K1) x 4(4:6:6:6)times, P2, K2, P18 (row 2 of giant braid cable), K2, P2, (K1, P1) x 4(4:6:6:6)times.

This sets the patt.

Keeping patt correct inc 1 st at both ends of next and every foll 4th(4th:6th:6th:6th) row until 56(58:62:64:68)sts.

Work straight until sleeve meas 15(18:21:24:27)cm/ 6(7:8¼:9½:10½)in, ending with RS facing for next row.

SHAPE TOP

Cast / bind off 3(4:5:5:5)sts at beg of next 2 rows. 50(50:52:54:58)sts.
Dec 1 st at both ends of next 4(5:5:6:7) rows. 42(40:42:42:44)sts.
Work 0(1:1:0:1) row.
Dec 1 st at both ends of next and every foll alt row until 24(24:24:24:24)st rem.
Work 1 row.
Cast / bind off 3 sts at beg of next 4 rows.
Cast / bind off rem 12(12:12:12:12)sts.

Join right shoulder seam

NECKBAND

Using 3.75mm/US 5 needles, RS of work facing and C, pick up and K 10(10:15:15:15)sts down side of neck, 20(24:26:26:28)sts from holder, 13(13:19:19:19)sts up side of neck, 26(30:30:34:36)sts from holder, and 3(3:4:4:4)down back neck. 72(80:94:98:102)sts.
Work 3cm/1¼ in in K1, P1 rib.
Cast / bind off in rib.

FINISH

Weave in any long ends. Gently steam on reverse. Sew left shoulder and neckband seam. Sew in sleeves. Sew sleeve and side seams.

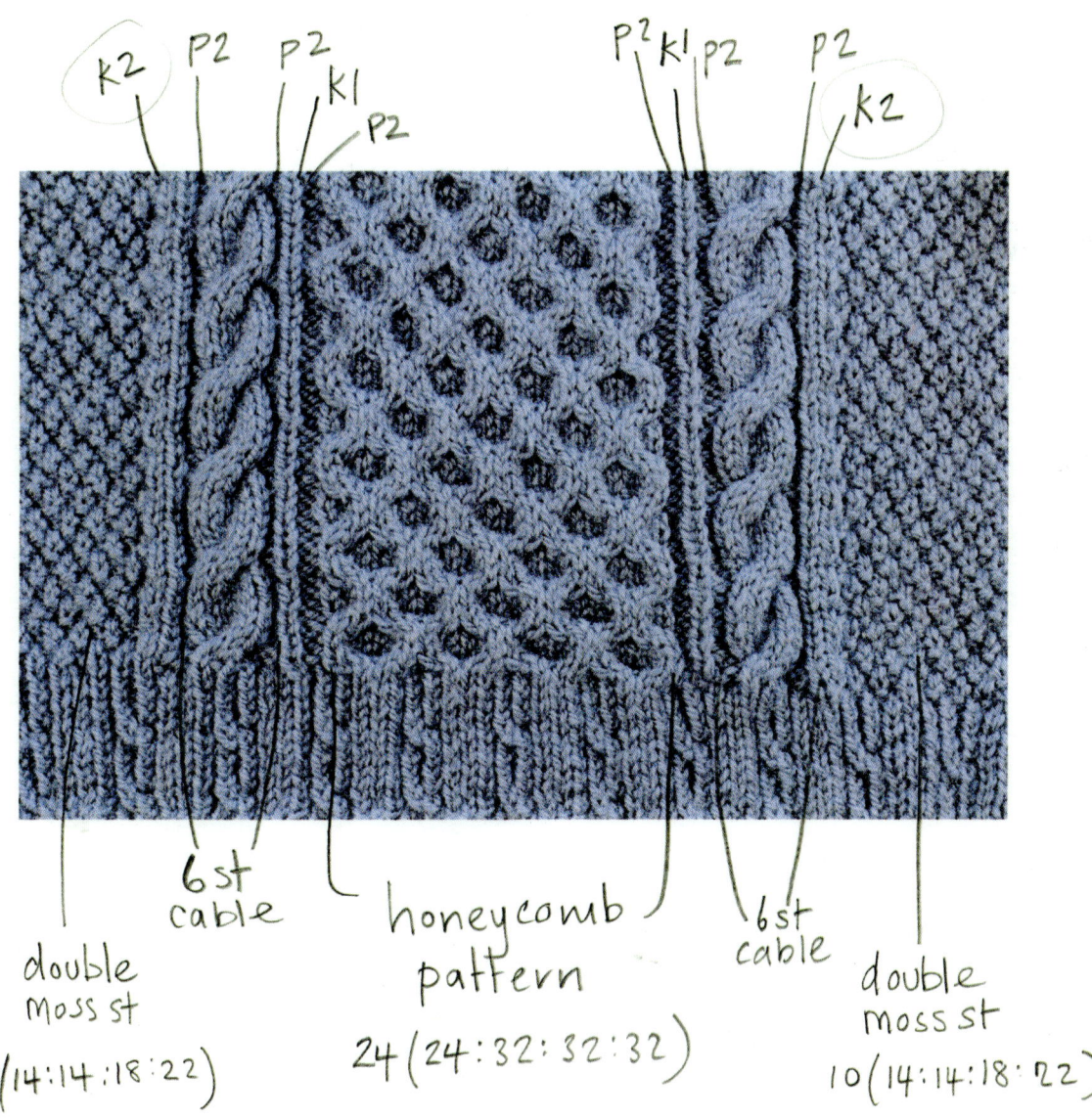

06. BALACLAVA

06. BALACLAVA

To keep ears cosy, a retro style balaclava given a contemporary look in micro stripes. Knitted in stocking / stockinette stitch with a rib trim.

MATERIALS
erika knight British blue wool 100% Bluefaced Leicester wool 55m / 60 yds – 25g ball
A – 1(1:1) balls
B – 1(1:1) ball
3.25mm / US 3 and 3.75mm / US 5 needles
stitch holders
large eyed blunt tipped sewing needle

MEASUREMENTS

Approx. age	3-6mths	6-12mths	1-2yrs
Head circumference	30cm/12in	32cm/12½in	34cm/13½in
Finished length	21cm/8¼in	22cm/8¾in	24cm/9½in

TENSION / GAUGE
23sts and 30 rows to 10cm/4in meas over St st using 3.75mm/US 5 needles. Change needle size if necessary to ensure the correct tension.

STRIPE SEQUENCE
2 rows A
2 rows B

MAKE
Using 3.25mm/US 3 needles and A cast on 67(71:79)sts and work in rib as foll:
Row 1(RS): (K1,P1) to last st, K1.
Row 2: (P1,K1) to last st, P1.
Rep last 2 rows another 7(8:9) times.
Next row: rib to last 9(9:11)sts and slip these sts onto a holder.
Next row: rib to last 9(9:11)sts and slip these sts onto another holder.

Change to 3.75mm/US 5 needles and starting with a K row, cont in St st and foll the stripe sequence above until work meas 19(20:22)cm/ 7½ (8:8¾)in from cast on edge, ending with RS facing for next row.

SHAPE CROWN
Row 1: K31(34:37), K2tog tbl, **TURN**.
Row 2: Sl1,P13(15:17), P2tog, **TURN**.
Row 3: Sl1,K13(15:17), K2tog tbl, **TURN**.
Rep last 2 rows until 15(17:19)sts rem. Leave sts on a holder.

Slip 9(9:11)sts on second holder onto a 3.25mm/US 3needle, then using yarn A pick up and K 30(33:38) sts along side of balaclava, 15(17:19)sts from holder, 30(33:38)sts along other side of balaclava, then rib as set across 9(9:11)sts on holder. 93(101:117)sts.

Using yarn A work 7(9:9) rows in rib. Cast / bind off using a 3.75mm/US 5 needle.

FINISH

Weave in any long ends. Gently steam on reverse, to enhance the yarn, avoiding the ribbing. Join neckband at front.

> generally pick up 3 sts out of every 4 sts

07. TIPPED TANK TOP

08. FURRY PARKA

08. FURRY PARKA

Parka-style coat made in natural fur wool. Knitted in garter stitch throughout with fish tail hem, hood and zip fastener detail – for your little mod!

MATERIALS
erika knight fur wool 97% British wool, 3% nylon binder, 40m/44yds -100g/3½ oz hank
4(5: 6) hanks
12mm / US 17 needles
25.5(30.5:35.5)cm / 10(12:14)in double - ended zip
Large eyed blunt tipped sewing needle

MEASUREMENTS

Approx. age	6-12mths	2-3yrs	4-5yrs
To fit chest	51-56cm/20-22in	56-61cm/22-24in	63-71cm/26-28in
Finished size	56cm/22in	61cm/24in	71cm/28in
Chest flat	28cm/11in	30cm /12in	35cm/14in
Front length	33cm/13in	38cm/15in	43cm/17in
Back length	43cm/17in	50cm/20in	57cm/22½in
Sleeve length	20cm/8in	23cm/9in	26cm/10in

TENSION / GAUGE
6.5 sts and 10 rows to 10cm / 4in meas over g stitch using 12mm / US 17 needles. Change needle size if necessary to ensure the correct tension.

MAKE

BACK
Cast on 8(8:10)sts and work in g st throughout as foll:
Knit 2 rows.
Cast on 2 sts at beg of next 6(8:8)rows. 20(24:26)sts.
Largest size only: Cast on 1 st at beg of next 2 rows. 20(24:28)sts
Place markers at both ends of last row to show start of side seam.
Cont straight until work meas 10(11.5:13) cm/4(4½ :5¼)in from markers.
Dec 1 st at both ends of next row. 18(22:26)sts
Cont straight until work meas 17(20:23) cm/6¾ (8:9)in from markers

SHAPE ARMHOLES
Cast / bind off 2(2:2)sts at beg of next 2 rows. 14(18:22)sts.
Work straight until armhole meas 13(15:17)cm / 5¼ (6: 6¾)in

SHAPE BACK NECK AND SHOULDERS
Next row: K5(6:8), **TURN**.
Next row: Cast / bind off 2 sts at beg of next row.
Cast / bind off rem 3(4:6)sts.
Re-join yarn to rem sts and cast / bind off centre 4(6:6)sts, K to end of row.
Next row: K
Next row: cast / bind off 2 sts, K to end of row.
Cast / bind off rem 3(4:6)sts.

FRONTS - BOTH THE SAME

Cast on 11(13:15)sts and work 10(11.5:13)cm/4(4½ :5¼)in, in g st.
Dec 1 st at end of next row, placing marker at the end of this row to mark the dec. 10(12:14)sts.
Cont straight until work meas 17(20:23)cm/6¾ (8:9)in from cast on edge, ending on the same edge as the marker.

SHAPE ARMHOLE

Cast / bind off 2 sts at beg of next row. 8(10:12)sts.
Work straight until armhole meas 10(12:14)cm/ 4(4¾ : 5½)in ending at centre front edge.

SHAPE NECK

Next row: Cast / bind off 3(4:4)sts at beg of row. 5(6:8) sts.
Dec 1 st at neck edge on next 2 rows. 3(4:6)sts.
K 2 rows straight.
Cast / bind off rem 3(4:6)sts.

SLEEVES

Cast on 14(14:16)sts and inc 1 st at both ends of every 4th row until 20(22:24)sts.
Work straight until sleeve meas 18(21:24)cm/ 7(8¼: 9½)in from cast on edge. Place markers at both ends of last row.
Work 2 rows straight.
Cast / bind off loosely.

HOOD

Cast on 24(26:26)sts and work 8(10:10) rows g st.
Next row: K6, inc in next st, K to last 7 sts, inc in next st, K to end. 26(28:28)sts
Work 4 rows straight.
Next row: K6, inc in next st, K to last 7 sts, inc in next st, K to end. 28(30:30)sts
Work 5 rows straight.
Shape top
Next row: K17(18:18), K2tog, turn.
Next row: Sl 1, K6, K2tog, turn.
Rep last row until 8 sts rem.
Cast / bind off tightly.

FINISH

Weave in any long ends. Join shoulders. Sew in sleeves, matching markers to side seams. Sew side and sleeve seams. Sew on hood.

Sew on zip to RS of the parka, along the centre front.

09. ROMPER

09. ROMPER

Knitted in stocking / stockinette stitch with rib trims and a little bib with simple shaping and integral straps. Once retro, the romper suit looks contemporary again and super cute layered over leggings.

MATERIALS
erika knight British blue wool 100% Bluefaced Leicester wool 55m / 60 yds – 25g ball
4(4:5) balls
3.25 / US 3 and 3.75mm / US 5 needles
stitch holder
spool of shirring elastic
2 buttons
large eyed blunt tipped sewing needle

MEASUREMENTS

Approx. age	3-6mths	6-12mths	1-2 yrs
Width at widest point	28cm/11in	29/11½ in	30cm/12in
Length - top of waistband to bottom of rib cuff	16.5cm /6½in	18cm/7in	19cm /7½in
Length of bib	9cm/3½in	10cm/4in	11cm/4½in

TENSION / GAUGE
23 stitches and 30 rows to 10cm / 4in meas over St st using 3.75mm / US 5 needles. Change needle size if necessary to ensure the correct tension.

MAKE

BACK
*Using 3.75mm / US 5 needles cast on 19(19:19)sts.

SHAPE LEGS AND CROTCH
Row 1: K
Row 2: Cast on 6(6:6) sts and P all sts.
Row 3: Cast on 6(6:6) sts and K these 6 sts, K2tog tbl, K15, K2 tog, K to end.
Row 4: Cast on 6(6:6) sts and P all sts.
Row 5: Cast on 6(6:6) sts and K these 6 sts, K6, K2tog tbl, K13, K2 tog, K to end.
Row 6: Cast on 9(9:9) sts and P all sts.
Row 7: Cast on 9(9:9) sts, K these 9 sts, K12, K2tog tbl, K11, K2 tog, K to end.
Row 8: Cast on 9(9:9) sts and P all sts.
Row 9: Cast on 9(9:9) sts and K these 9 sts, K21, K2tog tbl, K9, K2 tog, K to end.
Row 10: Cast on 2(3:4) sts and P all sts.
Row 11: Cast on 2(3:4) sts, K these 2(3:4) sts, K30, K2tog tbl, K7, K2 tog, K to end. 73(75:77) sts.
Row 12: P.
Place a marker at both ends of last row.
Row 13: K32(33:34) sts, K2tog tbl, K5, K2 tog, K to end.
Row 14: P
Row 15: K32(33:34) sts, K2tog tbl, K3,

K2 tog, K to end.
Row 16: P
Row 17: K32(33:34) sts, K2tog tbl, K1, K2 tog, K to end.
Row 18: P
Row 19: K32(33:34) sts, Sl 1, K2tog, psso, K to end. 65(67:69) sts
Row 20: P

Cont straight in St st until work meas 12.5(13.5: 14.5)cm / 5(5 ½ : 6)in from markers ending with RS facing for next row.*

SHAPE BACK

Row 1: K56(58:60) sts, **TURN**.
Row 2: P47(49:51) sts, **TURN**.
Row 3: K37(39:41) sts, **TURN**.
Row 4: P27(29:31) sts, **TURN**.
Row 5: K17(19:21) sts, **TURN**.
Row 6: P7(9:11) sts, **TURN**.
Row 7: K to end.
Row 8: P all sts.
**Change to 3.25mm / US 3 needles and work waistband as foll:
Row 1: (K1, P1) to last st, K1.
Row 2: (P1, K1) to last st, P1.
Rep last 2 rows four times. 10 rows rib worked**.
Cast / bind off.

FRONT

Work as back from * to * and from ** to **.

SHAPE BIB

Next row: Cast / bind off first 16(16:16) sts in rib, rib next 7 sts as set, K 17(19:21), rib as set to end of row.
Next row: Cast / bind off first 16(16:16) sts in rib, rib next 7 sts as set, P17(19:21), rib 8.
Next row: Rib 8, K17(19:21), rib 8.
Next row: Rib 8, P17(19:21), rib 8.
Rep last 2 rows 0(1:1) times.
Next row (dec): Rib 7, P2tog, K15(17:19), P2tog, rib 7.
Next row: Rib 8, P15(17:19), rib 8.
Next row: Rib 8, K15(17:19), rib 8.
Next row: Rib 8, P15(17:19), rib 8.
Rep last 2 rows once more.

Next row (dec): Rib 7, P2tog, K13(15:17), P2tog, rib 7.
Next row: Rib 8, P13(15:17), rib 8.
Next row: Rib 8, K13(15:17), rib 8.
Next row: Rib 8, P13(15:17), rib 8.
Rep last 2 rows once more.

Next row (dec): Rib 7, P2tog, K11(13:15), P2tog, rib 7.
Next row: Rib 8, P11(13:15), rib 8.
Next row: Rib 8, K11(13:15), rib 8.
Next row: Rib 8, P11(13:15), rib 8.
Rep last 2 rows once more.

Next row (dec): Rib 7, P2tog, K9(11:13), P2tog, rib 7.
Next row: Rib 8, P9(11:13), rib 8.
Next row: Rib 8, K9(11:13), rib 8.
Next row: Rib 8, P9(11:13), rib 8.
Rep last 2 rows 0(1:2) times.

Next row (RS): (K1, P1) to last st, K1.
Next row: (P1: K1) to last st, P1.
Rep last two rows 1(2:2) times. 4(6:6) rows worked.

STRAPS

Rib first 8 sts and place on a holder, cast / bind off next 9(11:13) sts in rib, rib to end. Work 20(23:26)cm / 8(9:10¼)in in rib as set on these last 8 sts.
Make buttonhole: Rib 3, cast / bind off next 2 sts, rib to end.
Next row: Rib 3, cast on 2 sts, rib to end. Work a further 2.5(2.5:2.5)cm / 1(1:1) in.

Cast / bind off in rib.

With RS of work facing slip sts on holder onto needle and work to match first strap.

POCKET – MAKE ONE
Using 3.75mm / US 5 needles cast on 3(5:5)sts.
K one row.
Next row: P2, M1, P to last 2 sts, M1, P2.
Next row: K2, M1, K to last 2 sts, M1, P2.
Rep last two rows until 13(15:15) sts.
Cont straight until work meas 3(4:5)cm / 1¼(1½:2)in ending RS facing for next row.
Change to 3.25mm / US 3 needles and work in rib as foll.
Row 1: (K1, P1) to last st K1.
Row 2: (P1, K1) to last st P1.
Rep last 2 rows twice for all sizes.
6 rows worked.
Cast / bind off in rib.

NEXT
Weave in any long ends. Gently steam work to enhance the yarn. Join crotch seam using mattress stitch.

LEG BANDS
With RS of work facing and 3.25 mm / US 3 needles pick up and K64(66:68) sts evenly around leg shaping and work 5 rows in K1, P1 rib. Cast / bind off in rib. Repeat for other leg.

FINISH
Join side seams. Sew on pocket to back or front of romper, as desired. Turn work inside out and sew shirring elastic through every other stitch and every other row of waistband. Sew on buttons.

> M1, Make 1
> With tip of needle lift strand between last stitch worked and next stitch on left-hand needle and knit into back of it to increase one stitch.

10. LEGGINGS

11. VARSITY CARDY

cute!

11. VARSITY CARDY

A retro inspired cardigan with patch pockets, zip fastening and garter stitch mini shawl collar. Knitted in super chunky maxi wool in vibrant colours with a varsity inspired stripe and bold number motif.

MATERIALS

erika knight Maxi wool 100% pure wool 80m/87yds - 100g / 3oz hank
A - 2(2:3:4:5) hanks
B - 1(1:1:1:1) hanks
C - small amount for Swiss embroidery number motif
10mm /US 15 needles
Open-ended zip 20(20:25:30:30)cm / 8(8:10:12:12)in to match or clash in colour
Large eyed blunt tipped sewing needle

MEASUREMENTS

Approx age	3-6mths	6-12mths	1-2yrs	2-3 yrs	4-5 yrs
Chest	54cm/21½in	60cm/24in	66cm/26in	72cm/28½in	78cm/30¾in
Length	25cm/10in	33cm/13in	36cm/14in	42cm/16½in	46cm/18in
Sleeve Seam	20cm/8in	23cm/9in	25.5cm/10in	28cm/11in	30.5cm/12in

TENSION / GAUGE

10 sts and 12 rows to 10cm / 4in mea over St st using 10 mm/US 15 needles. Change needle size if necessary to ensure the correct tension.

MAKE

BACK

Using A cast on 26(30:34:38:42)sts and work 4(4:6:6:6)rows in K1, P1 rib.
Beg with a K row work 11(13:15:17:19) rows in St st.
Change to B and work 7(7:9:9:9) rows in St st.

SHAPE ARMHOLES

Cast/ bind off 2 sts at beg of next 2 rows. 22(26:30:34:38)sts.
Next row: K2, K2tog, K to last 4 sts, K2tog tbl, K2. 20(24:28:32:36)sts

1st and 2nd sizes only – change to A

ALL SIZES:
Next row: P.
Next row: K2, K2tog, K to last 4sts, K2tog tbl, K2. 18(22:26:30:34)sts.

3rd, 4th and 5th sizes only – change to A

ALL SIZES:
Work 7(9:11:13:17) rows in St st, ending with RS facing for next row.

SHAPE SHOULDERS
Cast/bind off 4(5:6:7:8)sts at beg of next 2 rows.
Cast/bind off rem 10(12:14:16:18)sts.

LEFT FRONT
Using A cast on 14(16:18:20:22)sts and work 4(4:6:6:6)rows in rib with g st edge as foll:
Row 1(RS): (K1, P1) to last 2 sts, K2.
Row 2: K2, (K1, P1) to end of row.

Cont in St st with g st edge as foll:
Next row: K.
Next row: K2, P to end.
Work a further 9(11:13:15:17) rows.
Change to B and work 7(7:9:9:9) rows, ending with RS facing for next row.

SHAPE ARMHOLE
Cast/ bind off 2 sts at beg of next row. 12(14:16:18:20)sts
Next row: K2, P to end.
Next row: K2, K2tog, K to end.

1st and 2nd sizes only – change to A

ALL SIZES:
Rep last 2 rows once more.
10(12:14:16:18)sts

3rd, 4th and 5th sizes only change to A

ALL SIZES:
Work 2(2:2:6:8) rows with g st edge, ending with WS facing for next row.

SHAPE NECK
Cast / bind off 3(3:3:4:4)sts at beg of row. 7(9:11:12:14)sts
Next row: K.
Next row: Cast / bind off 2(3:2:2:3)sts at beg of row. 5(6:9:10:11)sts
Next row: K to last 4 sts, K2tog tbl, K2. 4(5:8:9)sts
Next row: P.

1st and 2nd sizes only: Cast / bind off rem 4(5) sts

3rd, 4th and 5th sizes only
Next row: K to last 4 sts, K2tog tbl, K2. (7:8:9)sts
Next row: P.
Next row: K to last 4 sts, K2tog tbl, K2. (6:7:8)sts
Next row: P.
Cast/ bind off rem (6:7:8)sts.

RIGHT FRONT
Using A cast on 14(16:18:20:22)sts and work 4(4:6:6:6)rows in rib with g st edge as foll:
Row 1(RS): K2, (P1, K1) to end of row.
Row 2: (P1, K1) to last 2 sts, K2.

Cont in St with g st edge as foll:
Next row: K.
Next row: P to last 2 sts, K2.

Work a further 9(11:13:15:17) rows.
Change to B and work 8(8:10:10:10) rows, ending with WS facing for next row.

SHAPE ARMHOLE

Cast/ bind off 2 sts at beg of next row, P to last 2 sts, K2. 12(14:16:18:20)sts
Next row: K to last 4 sts, K2tog tbl, K2. 11(13:15:17:19)sts.

1st and 2nd sizes only change to A.

ALL SIZES:
Next row: P to last 2 sts, K2.
Next row: K to last 4 sts, K2tog tbl, K2. 10(12:14:16:18)sts.

3rd, 4th and 5th sizes only change to A

ALL SIZES:
Work 3(3:3:7:9) rows with g st edge, ending with RS facing for next row.

SHAPE NECK

Cast/ bind off 3(3:3:4:4)sts at beg of row. 7(9:11:12:14) sts
Next row: P.
Next row: Cast/ bind off 2(3:2:2:3)sts at beg of row. 5(6:9:10:11)sts
Next row: P.
Next row: K2, K2tog, K to end. 4(5:8:9:10)sts

1st and 2nd sizes only: Cast/ bind off rem 4(5) sts.

3rd, 4th and 5th sizes only

Next row: P.
Next row: K2, K2tog, K to end. (7:8:9)sts
Next row: P.
Next row: K2, K2tog, K to end. (6:7:8)sts
Cast/ bind off rem (6:7:8) sts

SLEEVES

Using A cast on 14(16:18:20:22)sts and work 4(4:6:6:6)rows in K1, P1 rib. Starting with a K row, cont in St st, inc one st at both ends of every 4th(5th:5th:5th:6th) row as foll until 22(24:26:28:30)sts.

Inc on a RS row: K2, M1, K to last 2 sts, M1, K2.
Inc on a WS row: P2, M1, P to last 2 sts, M1, P2.

AT THE SAME TIME change to B on row 14(16:14:16:18) and work 7(7:9:9:9) rows ending with RS facing for next row.

SHAPE TOP

Cast/ bind off 2 sts at beg of next 2 rows. 18(20:22:24:26)sts.
Next row: K2, K2tog, K to last 4 sts, K2tog tbl, K2. 16(18:20:22:24)sts

1st and 2nd sizes only: change to A

ALL SIZES:
Next row: P.
Next row: K2, K2tog, K to last 4 sts, K2tog tbl, K2. 14(16:18:20:22)sts
Next row: P.

1st size only

Cast/ bind off 2 sts at beg of next 4 rows. Cast/ bind off rem 6 sts

2nd size only

Next row: K2, K2tog, K to last 4 sts, K2tog tbl, K2. 14 sts
Next row: P
Cast/ bind off 2 sts at beg of next 4 rows. Cast/ bind off rem 6 sts.

3rd size only
Change to A
Next row: K2, K2tog, K to last 4 sts, K2tog tbl, K2. 16 sts
Next row: P.
Next row: K2, K2tog, K to last 4 sts, K2tog tbl, K2. 14 sts
Cast/ bind off 2 sts at beg of next 4 rows.
Cast/ bind off rem 6 sts.

4th and 5th sizes only
Change to A
Next row: K2, K2tog, K to last 4 sts, K2tog tbl, K2. (18:20)sts
Dec 1 st as above at both ends of foll 4th row. (16:18) sts
Next row: P.
Cast/ bind off 2 sts at beg of next 4 rows.
Cast/ bind off rem (8:10)sts

PATCH POCKETS (MAKE 2 THE SAME)
Using A cast on 7(8:9:9:10)sts and work in St st for 6(8:8:10:10) rows, ending RS facing.
Next row: P.
Next row: K.
Next row: P.
Cast/ bind off

COLLAR
Using A cast on 3(3:4:4:4)sts and work in g st as foll:
Inc 1 st at both ends of next and every foll alt row until 7(7:10:10:10)sts.
Work 1 row.
Inc 1 st at **BEG** of next and every foll **ALT** row until 11(11:14:14:14)sts.
Work 25(29:31:35:39) rows straight.
Dec 1 st at **BEG** of next and every foll **ALT** row until 7(7:10:10:10)sts.
Work 1 row.
Dec 1 st at both ends of next and every foll **ALT** row until 3(3:4:4:4)sts rem.
Cast/ bind off.

MAKE
Weave in any long ends. Lay work out flat and gently steam to enhance the yarn. Oversew shoulder seams. Sew sleeves into armholes. Sew side and sleeve seams. Pin and tack zip into position along the length of the front under the g st edge, easing to fit. Sew in zip using backstitch.
Find centre back of collar by folding in half lengthways and pin to centre back neck. Pin around neck, with cast on and cast off edges along the front neck cast off edges. Oversew into position and fold collar over. Sew pockets onto fronts.

EMBROIDER
With C 'Swiss embroider' (see workshop page 80-81) the number of your choice over the centre colour band on the back. Refer to the small size number charts for the 1st and 2nd sizes and to the large size number charts for the 3rd, 4th and 5th sizes. Position the number over the centre of the colour band, placing the number approx. 2(2:4:4:4) rows at top and bottom of colour band.

CHARTS (SMALL NUMBERS)

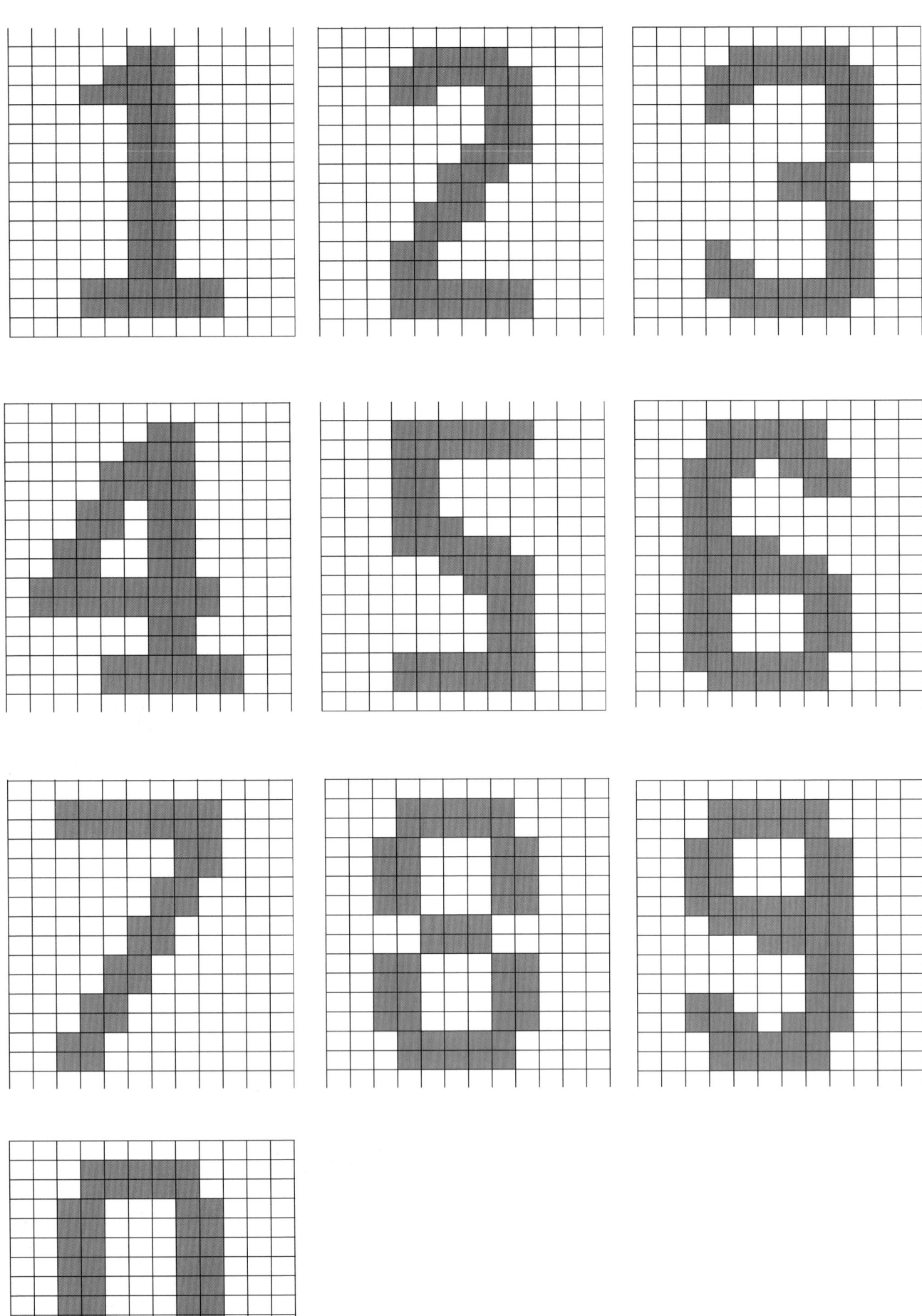

CHARTS (LARGE NUMBERS)

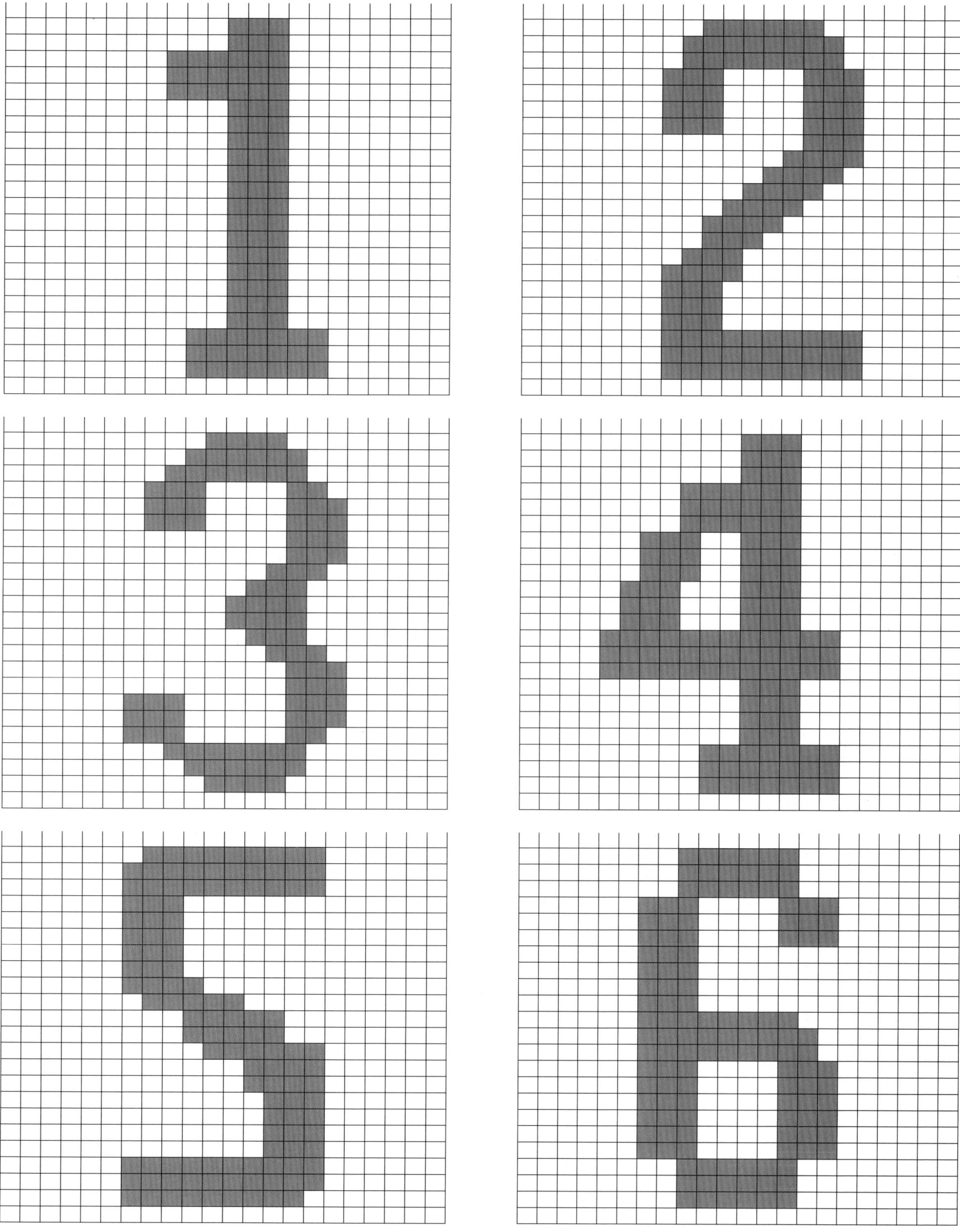

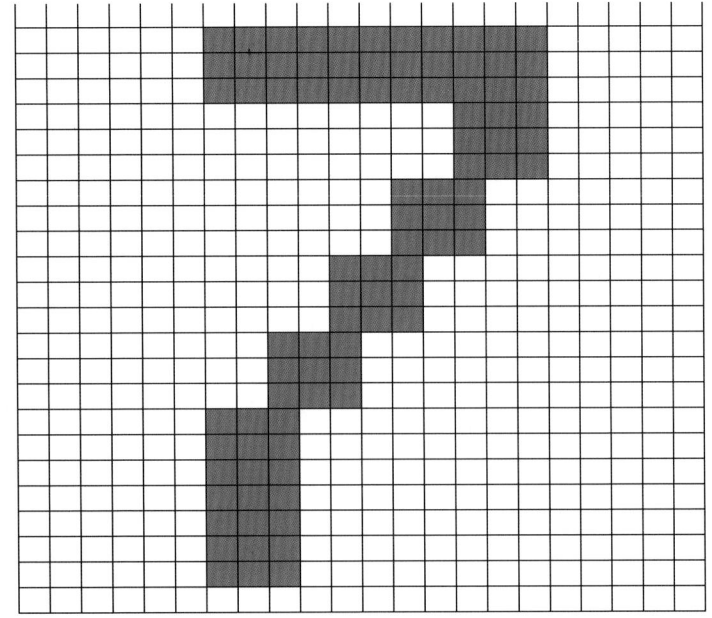
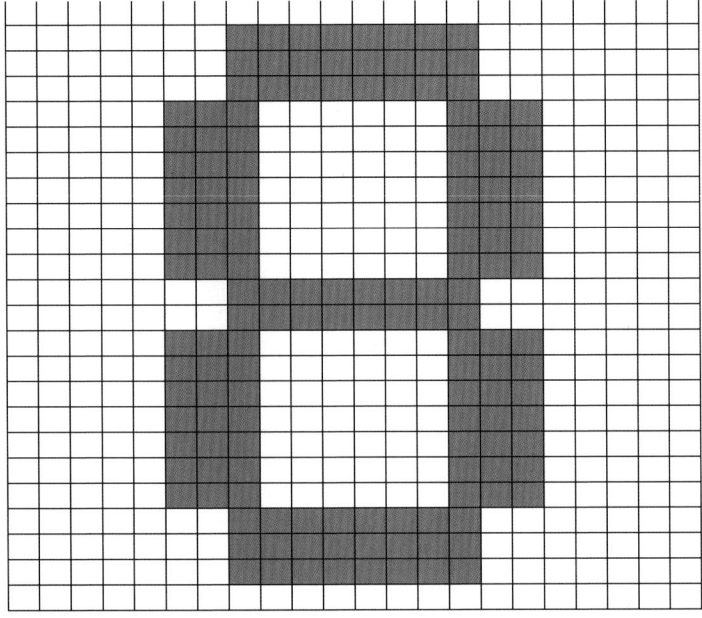
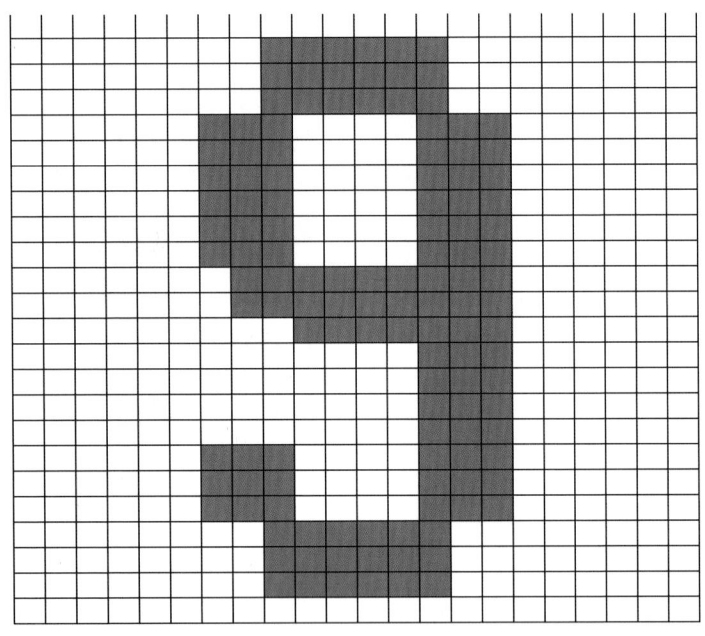
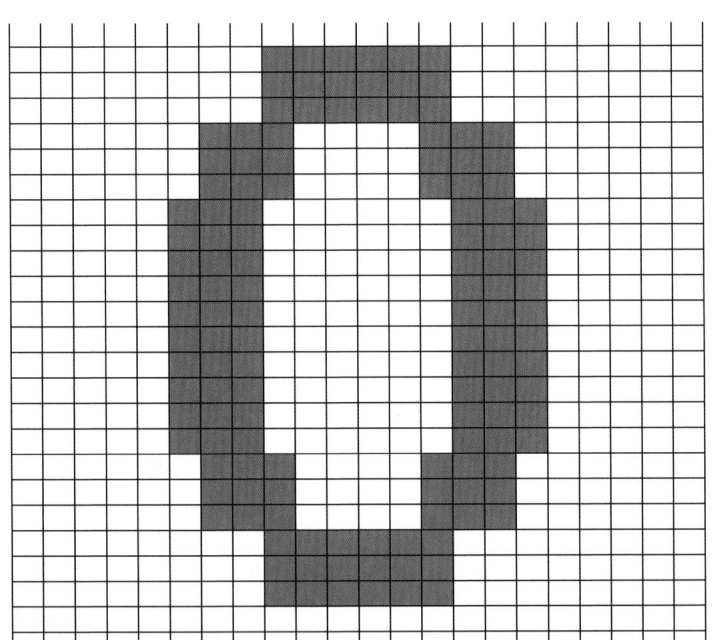

70

12. SCRAP BANDIT

12. SCRAP BANDIT

A simple toy knitted using scraps of wool from other projects and filled with a little bean bag. Knitted from the top of his head to the tip of his feet with a striped body and intarsia and Swiss embroidery details.

MATERIALS
erika knight British blue wool 100% Bluefaced Leicester wool, 55m/60yds – 25g ball
A 1 ball
B 1 ball
C scrap
D scrap
E scrap
3.25mm / US 3 needles
stitch holder
large eyed blunt tipped sewing needle
small piece of fabric - felt or fur for ears
small piece of cotton approx. 50 x 30cm / 20 x 12in to make bag for dried beans
approx. 200g / 7oz dried beans
(we used lentils)

MEASUREMENTS
One size approx. 34cm / 13½ in long and 10cm / 4in wide

TENSION / GAUGE
25 sts and 33 rows to 10 cm / 4in meas over St st with 3.25 mm/US 3 needles. Change needle size if necessary, to ensure the correct tension. A smaller sized needle is used to make a firm fabric.

NOTES
Striping or joining in a new ball- on row before you need the new colour, work to the last stitch.
Taking the end of the new colour, use together with the yarn in work to work the last stitch, creating a 'double stitch'
On the first stitch of next row, work the double stitch as one stitch with just the end of the new colour. This will securely 'anchor' your new yarn and not create unsightly knots nor create bumps.

MAKE

BACK
Using A cast on 25sts and starting with a K row work in St st as foll.
3 rows A
3 rows B
3 rows A
1 row B
10 rows C
1 row A
3 rows B
3 rows A
3 rows B
3 rows A
3 rows B
3 rows A
3 rows B
3 rows A
3 rows B
3 rows A
3 rows B
3 rows A

NOW WORK THE LEGS
The first leg is worked on the first 7 sts as foll:
Using D, P7, **TURN**, leaving rem sts on a holder.
Starting with a K row work 56 rows in St st using D.
Cast / bind off.

With WS of work facing slip sts from holder back onto a needle and using A cast / bind off centre 11 sts purlwise. Change to C, and P to end of row. (7 sts).
Starting with a K row work 56 rows in St st using C.
Cast / bind off

FRONT
Using A cast on 25sts and starting with a K row work in St st as foll.
3 rows A
3 rows B
3 rows A
1 row B
2 rows C
Next row: 5C, 6A, 3C, 6A, 5C
Next row: 5C, 4A, 7C, 4A, 5C
Next row: 5C, 2A, 11C, 2A, 5C
Next row: 1 row C
Next row: 12C, 1B, 12C
Next row: 10C, 5B, 10C
Next row: 7C, 11A, 7C
Next row: 5C, 15A, 5C
1 row A
3 rows B
3 rows A
3 rows B
3 rows A
3 rows B
3 rows A
3 rows B
3 rows A
3 rows B
3 rows A
3 rows B
3 rows A

NOW WORK THE LEGS
The first leg is worked on the first 7 sts as foll:
Using C, P7 sts, **TURN**, leaving rem sts on a holder.

Starting with a K row work 56 rows in St st using C

Cast / bind off.

With WS of work facing slip sts from holder back onto a needle and using A cast / bind off centre 11 sts purlwise. Change to D and P to end of row. (7 sts).
Starting with a K row work 56 rows in St st using D.
Cast / bind off.

ARMS - MAKE 2 - ONE USING D AND ONE USING E
Using D or E, cast on 10 sts and starting with a K row, work 34 rows in St st. Cast / bind off.

FINISH
Weave in any long ends. Gently steam work on reverse. Pin the front and back pieces together with WS facing. Over sew down body and around legs, sew across bottom of body, leaving the top of the head open.

MAKE BEAN BAG
Cut 2 pieces from cotton fabric 20 x 11cm / 8 x 4 ¼ in. Sew round three sides. Turn inside out and press. Fill with dried beans and sew last seam.
Insert bean bag into head opening.
Over sew across top of head.
Fold arms in half length ways and over sew around all edges. Position and sew to body.
Embroider eyes with Swiss-embroidery or French knot.

Ears
Cut ears from desired fabric as per the template, sew onto corners of head.

TEMPLATES

template for ears cut x 4

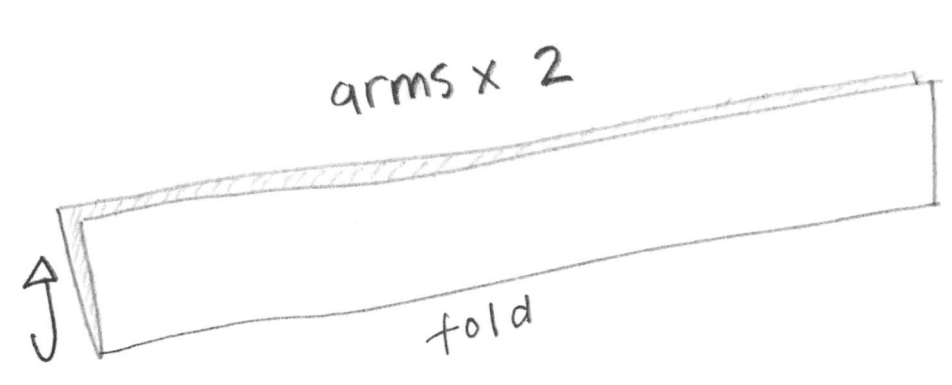

SAFETY NOTE
It is very important when making anything for little children to keep safety in mind. We recommend that this toy is not suitable for children under 3 years. Make sure your scrap bandit is sewn up securely so that no beans may escape. You could replace beans with washable toy stuffing, which conforms to safety standards. Always check for any stray pins or needles that may have been used in making, before you give this toy to a child.

Basic Info

TENSION / GAUGE

Achieving the correct tension can really make the difference in creating a successful garment. The tension determines both the shape and size of the knitting so any variation, however small, can distort the finished garment. Different designers and yarns will have different tensions, so it is important that you match the tension given at the start of each pattern. I recommend that you knit a 10cm/4in square in the pattern or stitch given in the tension/gauge instruction of the pattern and measure the number of stitches you have per row. If you have too many stitches or too few stitches, try knitting another square using larger or smaller needles. Once you have achieved the correct tension you will be able to knit your garment to the measurements provided in the pattern.

SKILL LEVELS

In reality, all the projects in this book are unashamedly simple – that's my style. However, each project has been attributed with a skill level in accordance with the Craft Yarn Council of America's rating system in order to let you know what techniques you are mastering.

beginner ✶
Beginner projects - for first time knitters using basic knit and purl stitches. Minimal shaping.

easy ✶✶
Easy projects - using basic stitches, repetitive stitch patterns, simple colour changes and simple shaping and finishing, such as picking up stitches.

intermediate ✶✶✶
Intermediate projects – with a variety of stitches, such as basic cables, simple intarsia, mid-level shaping and finishing such as short row shaping and Swiss embroidery/ duplicate stitch.

experienced ✶✶✶✶
Experienced projects – using advanced techniques and stitches such as short rows, fairisle, more intricate intarsia, cables, lace patterns and numerous colour changes

YARN

The designs in this book have been created with a certain yarn in mind. Careful consideration has been given to the effect of the weight, meterage/yardage, quality and colours of the chosen yarns on the finished garment. Please bear this mind if you wish to substitute any of the suggested yarns for an alternative. The amount of yarn given in each pattern is based on the average requirements and is an approximate guide. When purchasing yarn for your project ensure that you buy sufficient, and in the same dye lot to ensure colour continuity (note that yarns are dyed in small batches and therefore the same dye lot may not be available at a later date).

TENSION / GAUGE

23 sts and 30 rows to 10cm / 4in meas over St st using 3.75 mm/US 5 needles. Change needle size, if necessary, to ensure the correct tension.

Abbvs

The following is a list of the most commonly used abbreviations within the knitting patterns in this book. In addition, special abbreviations may also be included at the start of each pattern.

[ ]	work instructions within square brackets as many time as directed
( )	work instructions with round brackets for your chosen size
*	repeat instructions following the single asterisk as directed
**	repeat instructions up to or following the double asterisks as directed
alt	alternate
approx.	approximately
beg	begin/ beginning
bet	between
cm	centimetre(s)
cont	continue / continuing
dec	decrease / decreases / decreasing
foll	follow/ follows / following
g	gram(s)
inc	increase/ increases / increasing
k or K	knit
k1b	knit into stitch below next st
g st	garter stitch, every row knit
k2tog	knit 2 stitches together
k2tog tbl	knit 2 stitches together through back loops
kb1	knit into back of next stitch
kfb	knit into front and back of next stitch
kwise	knitwise
LH	left hand
m	metre(s)
M1	make one – a knitwise increase
M1 p-st	make one – a purlwise increase
mm	millimeter(s)
oz	ounce(s)
p or P	purl
patt(s)	pattern(s)
p2tog	purl 2 stitches together
p2tog tbl	purl 2 stitches together through back loops
psso	pass slipped stitch over
pwise	purlwise
rem	remain / remains / remaining
rep	repeat / repeats / repeating
rev st st	reverse stocking stitch
RH	right hand
RS	right side
sl	slip
sl1k	slip 1 knitwise
sl1p	slip 1 purlwise
sl st	slip stitch(es)
ssk	slip, slip, knit these 2 stitches together – a one stitch decrease
sssk	slip, slip, slip, knit these 3 stitches together
st(s)	stitch(es)
St st	stocking stitch
tbl	through back loop
tog	together
WS	wrong side
yb	yarn back – as if to knit
yd(s)	yard(s)
yf	yarn forward – as if to purl
yo	yarn over

Terms

Alt rows this is used when you have to work something on every alternate row, most usually shaping.

At the same time used when you are shaping a garment and you need to do different shapings on different edges. For example, you may be decreasing for the armhole and at the same time decreasing for the neck.

Cast / bind off to finish off an edge and keep stitches from unraveling by lifting the first stitch over the second, the second over the third, and so on.

Cast / bind off in rib maintain the rib patterns as you cast off (knit the knit stitches; purl the purl stitches).

Cast on form a foundation row by making a specified number of loops on the knitting needle.

Cont in patt / as set continue to work in the pattern that has been established in the preceding rows.

Decrease reduce the number of stitches in a row (for example, knit 2 together; purl 2 together).

Increase add to the number of stitches in a row (for example, knit in front and back of stitch).

Make one with tip of needle, lift strand between last stitch worked and next stitch on left-hand needle and knit into back of it to increase one stitch.

On 4th and on every foll 6th row usually used for shaping: work three rows then work the decrease of increase (whichever is specified) on the fourth row. Work five more rows then decrease or increase as specified in the sixth row. You then continue to work five rows and increase or decrease on the sixth row until you have completed the required number of increases or decreases.

Place markers loop a piece of contrasting yarn or stitch marker onto the needle or ends of row.

Purlwise insert the needle into stitch as if you were going to purl it.

Rep from * repeat the instructions given after the *

Slip stitch pass a stitch from the left-hand to the right-hand needle as if to purl without working it.

Turn stop working at this point (ignore the stitches unworked on the left-hand needle), turn and work on these stitches as instructed.

Work straight/ even continue in specified pattern without increasing or decreasing.

Work to last 2 sts work across the row until there are two stitches (or number stated) on the left-hand needle.

Yarn over make a new stitch by placing the yarn over the right-hand needle (yfwd, yon, yrn).

NB! remember that when a knitting pattern refers to the left and right sides of an item it is referring to the left or right side as worn, rather than as you are looking at it.

Workshop

If you need a little bit more info on how to do something you may find it here! Techniques of putting colour in your knitting, such as colour blocking, stranding, Swiss embroidery and other stitches. Hopefully a little inspiration to personalise and further embellish your projects.

JOINING IN A NEW COLOUR

On row before you need the new colour, work to the last stitch. Taking the end of the new colour, use together with the yarn in work to work the last stitch, creating a 'double stitch'. On the first stitch of the next row, work the double stitch as one stitch with just the end of the new colour. This will securely 'anchor' your new yarn and not create unsightly knots nor create bumps.

THREE-NEEDLE CAST-OFF

The seam is worked on the right side of the knitting to form a decorative raised seam.

Knitting with colours

COLOUR BLOCKING

For working blocks of two or more colours, work in rows, joining in colours at appropriate point. Do not carry colours across wrong side of work, but link two colours by twisting round each other where they meet on wrong side to avoid a hole (see diagrams).

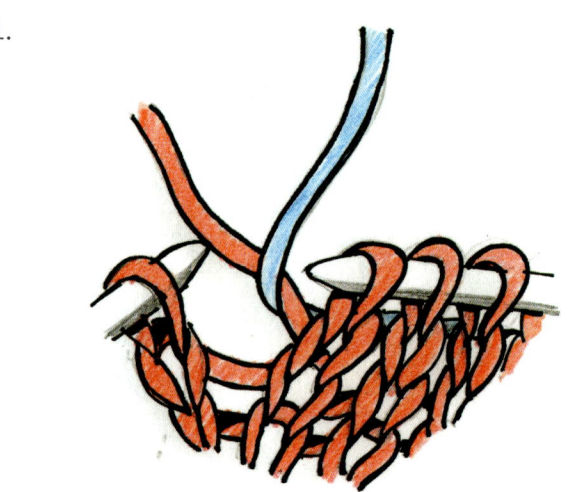

1.

1. Hold the needles with the stitches to be joined together with the wrong sides of the knitting facing each other. Insert a third needle through the centre of the first stitch on each needle and knit these two stitches together.

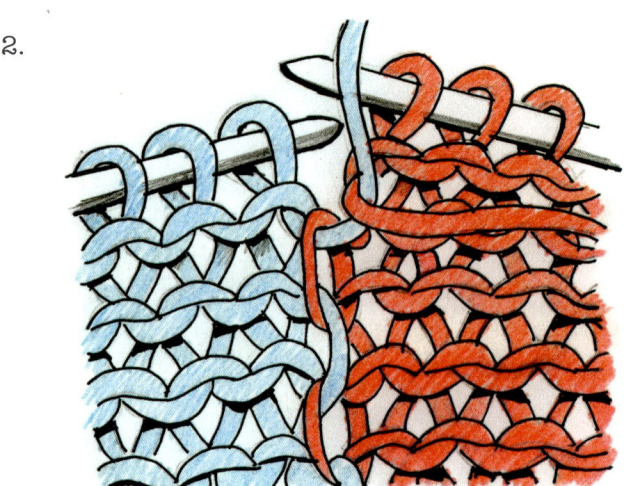

2.

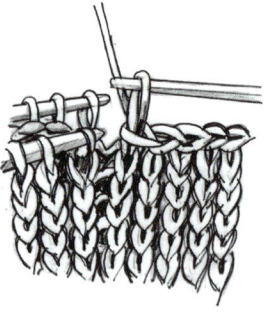

2. Continue to knit together one stitch from each needle as you cast / bind off the stitches in the usual way.

3. Open out the pieces of knitting, and you will see that this technique creates a 'raised chain' along the seam.

STRANDING AND WEAVING

The traditional method of using two colours is to strand a colour not in use at the back of the work. These designs are always worked in stocking stitch and the diagram shows how the stranding looks at the back of the work – wrong side. When carrying the wool over 6 or more stitches the strands will look long and unsightly. So, to avoid this appearance, simply twist the colour that is being stranded over the colour you are working in on every 3rd or 4th stitch.

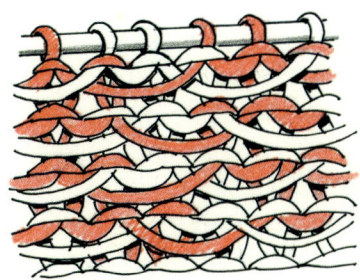

SWISS EMBROIDERY

An easy way to work a variety of coloured patterns on to a background of St st. Draw a design e.g. a motif, number of letter onto chart paper with each square representing one stitch. The pattern is worked so that each 'embroidered' stitch completely covers a knitted stitch with the new colour, blending in to look like the original knitting.

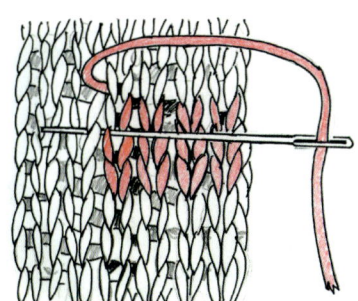 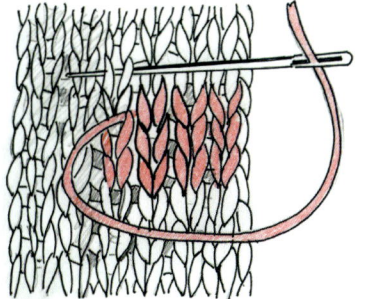

Using a large eyed blunt tipped needle and the colour required in a yarn of a similar weight to the knitting fasten in the yarn invisibly at the back. * Bring the needle up through centre of stitch from the back of the work, insert the needle from right to left, behind the stitch immediately above. Place needle down centre of original stitch and out through the centre of stitch to left, repeat from *. Always work stitches from right to left and from bottom to top working stitches vertically. It is easier to work the second and alternate rows if you turn the work upside down. This is so that the stitches are always worked in the same direction. On the front of the work, thread the needle under the two vertical loops of the same stitch, but one row below.

OVERCAST STITCH

Stitch over the edges of knitted fabric e.g. the legs and body of the scrap bandit toy to neaten a raw edge. Simply make an over and over stitch through both edges of your knitted fabric, keeping the stitches small and even.

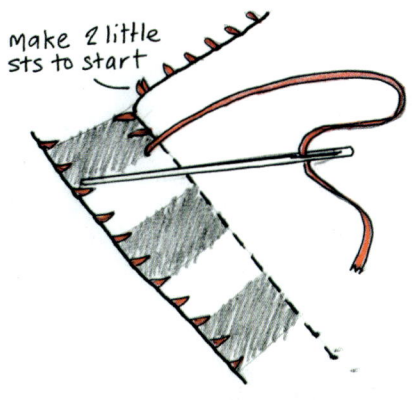

BLANKET STITCH

A great stitch for finishing edges and going round curves, use to join scribble sweater for a decorative edge or around scrap bandit toy.

To work the stitch, bring the thread to the right side on the lower line, then place the needle in position from the upper to the lower line (diagram). Make sure that the thread loop lies under the needle as shown.

Pull the stitch taut (but not too tight) to form a loop. Repeat as required.

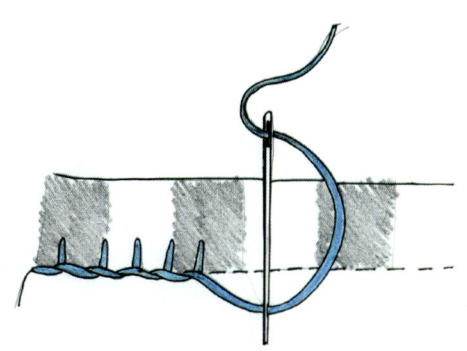

Finishing

When all the knitted pieces are done, take time to finish.

1. ends

Using a blunt tipped large eyed needle weave each end separately across the wrong side of the work (never along the edges) for about three or four stitches, then back one or two stitches, to hold the end firmly in place.

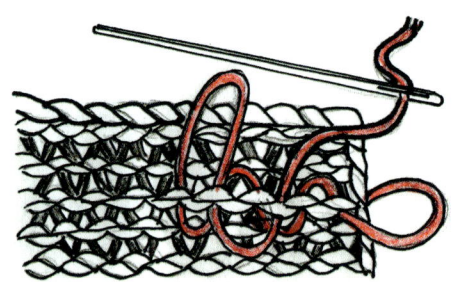

2. pin

Cover a table or other flat surface with a towel and lay each piece of knitting out flat with wrong side facing up. Make sure all the rows run in straight lines and check that the width and length of each piece matches the measurements given in the pattern. Pin closely to edge of each piece of knitting, placing pins at right angles to the edges. Use plenty of pins, placed close together to achieve a neat, straight edge.

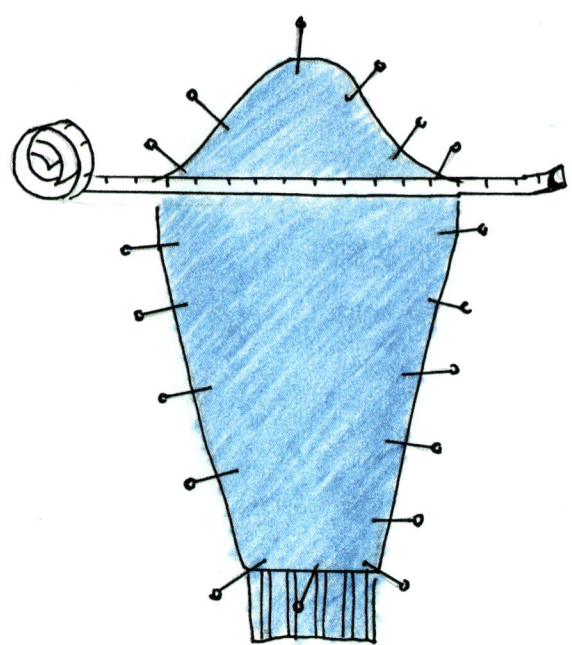

3. steam

Before you start, check for any specific instructions given in the pattern or printed on the yarn label. Erika Knight yarns are made with 100% natural wool and they are steamed during the spinning process so that all you need to do is cover your pinned, knitted pieces with a fine cotton cloth, such as a tea towel, set your iron to steam and hover over the knitted pieces, so that steam can permeate the cloth. Do not press the iron onto the knitted fabric. Note that rib edges, neckbands and any areas of garter stitch should not be steamed. Remove the cloth and allow knitting to dry before unpinning. If you are using an alternative yarn be sure to check the yarn label, and if in doubt, test steam your tension square before you steam your knitted pieces.

4. put pieces together

Refer to specific instructions in the pattern, but in general - join shoulder seams using either invisible stitch or back-stitch. Lay work out flat, and set in sleeve.

Square set in sleeve (Scribble Jumper)
Place centre of cast off edge of sleeves to shoulder seam. Set sleeve head into armhole, the straight sides at top of sleeve to form a neat rightangle to cast off stitches at armhole on front and back.

Shallow set in sleeve (Varsity Cardy, Colour Block Jumper)
Place centre of cast off edge of sleeve to shoulder seam, match decreases at beginning of armhole shaping to decreases at top of sleeve. Sew sleeve head into armhole, easing in shapings.

Join side and sleeve seams. Slip stitch any pockets into place. Sew on buttons to correspond with buttonholes, or sew in zip.

5. seam

Invisible stitch – joining two selvedges

Used to join all side and sleeve seams or where a flat seam with no bulk is required. Thread a large eyed blunt tipped needle with a length of yarn (this does not have to be the yarn you knitted with, as it will not show). With RS of both pieces facing, secure the yarn to edge of one piece. Take the needle across to the opposite edge, pick up the equivalent stitch on this piece, pull the yarn through: take the needle back to the first edge, returning the needle through hole of previous stitch, picking up the next stitch pull the yarn through. Continue in this way, picking up and pulling together stitch to stitch (row for row) along length of seam.

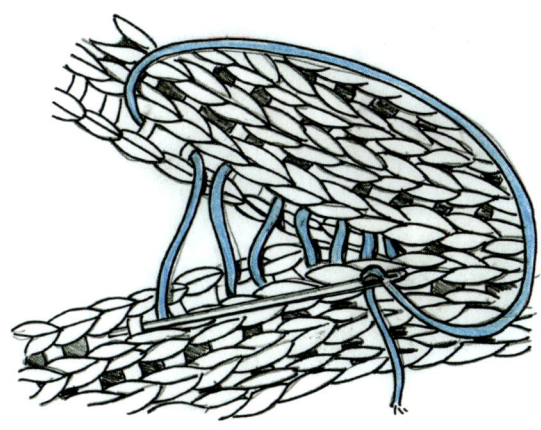

Invisible stitch – joining two cast/ bind off edges

1. Thread a large eyed blunt tipped needle with a length of yarn. With RS of both pieces facing, lay the two pieces to be joined with the cast off edges together. On the lower piece, from the back to the front, take the needle through the centre of the first stitch, just below the cast off edge. Next, take the needle through the centre of the first stitch on the upper piece and out through the centre of the next stitch.

2. Next, take the needle through the centre of the first stitch on the lower stitch again and out through the centre of the next stitch to the left. Continue in this way, switching from the lower piece to the upper piece, until the seam is complete.

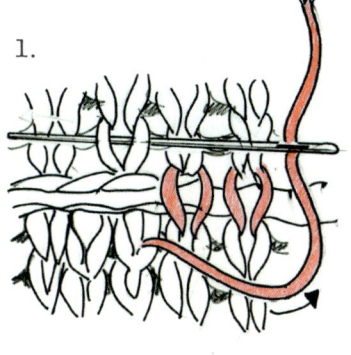 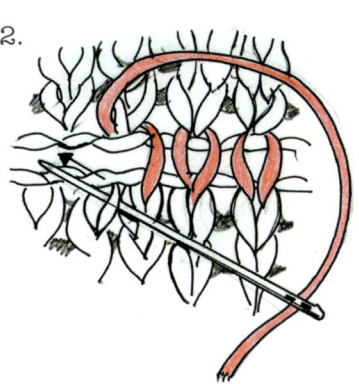

6. detail

Zips

Pin the zip to the opening, being sure that the knitting fits easily and is not wrinkled or stretched. The knitted edges should come right up to the teeth of the zip. Work in back stitch along the edges using a sewing thread. Be sure to choose a zip that is the correct weight for the garment.

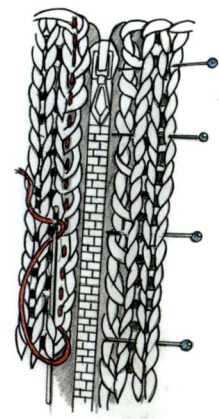

aftercare

When you have taken time to hand make your project or garment for your little one it makes sense to care for it, to keep it at its best for the next generation.
That's the best ethos for 'slow clothes'.

Check the ball band for wash care info.

Reshape your garments while they are still damp after washing and dry flat.

I recommend using Soak wash to care for your knitted garments. **www.soakwash.com**

Thanks to...

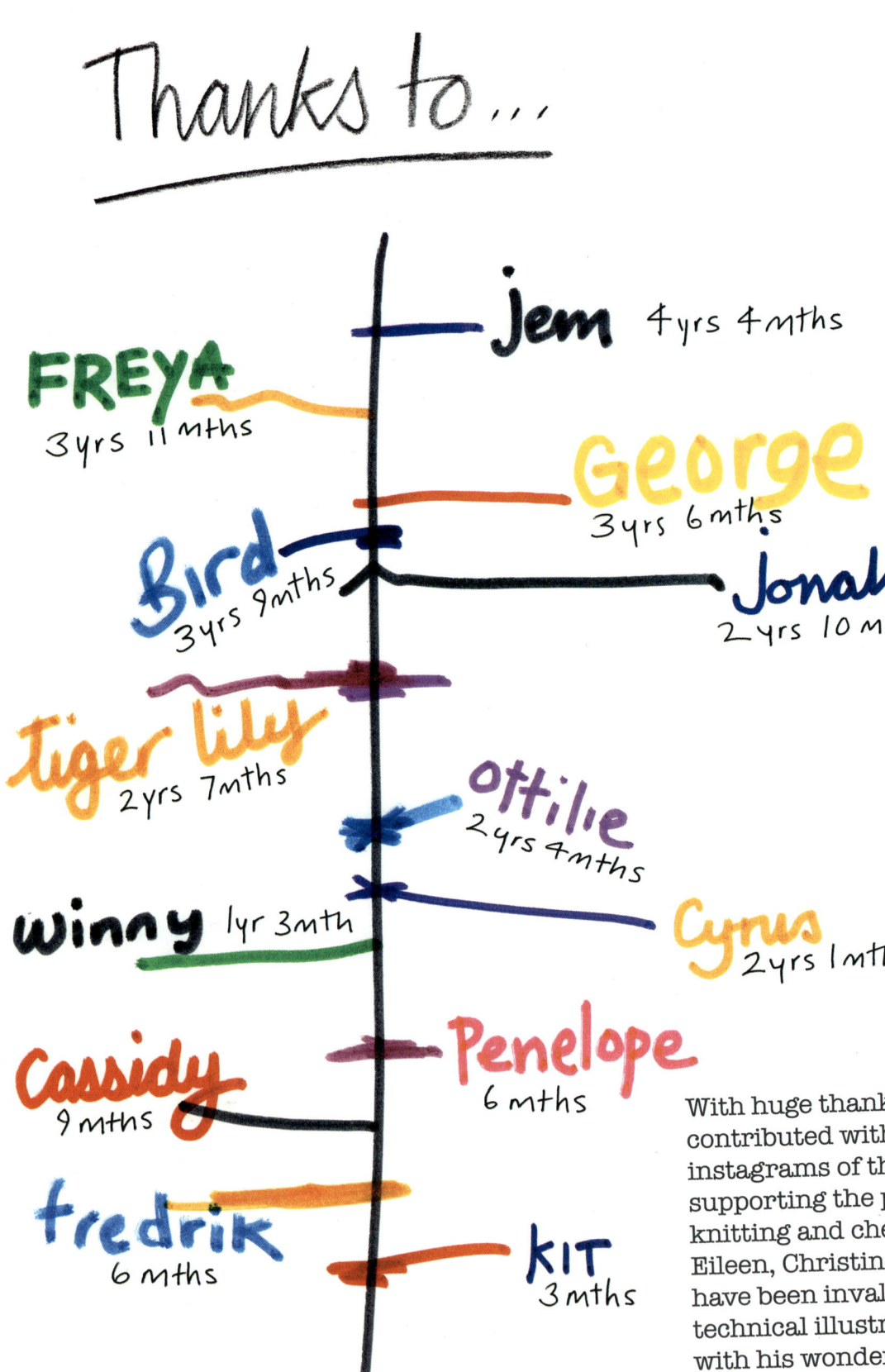

Jem 4yrs 4mths
FREYA 3yrs 11mths
George 3yrs 6mths
Bird 3yrs 9mths
Jonah 2yrs 10mths
Tiger lily 2yrs 7mths
Ottilie 2yrs 4mths
Winny 1yr 3mth
Cyrus 2yrs 1mth
Cassidy 9mths
Penelope 6mths
Fredrik 6mths
Kit 3mths

With huge thanks to all the Mums and Dads who contributed with photographs, snapshots and instagrams of their fab kids, to Darren Brant for supporting the project, Sally Lee for tirelessly knitting and checking and of course big thanks to Eileen, Christine and Julie whose knitting skills have been invaluable. Thanks also to Ian Harris for technical illustrations and to Arthur for inspiring us with his wonderful drawings.

You may wish to check out on Instagram:
@garlands.of.sweetpea
@ketchuponeverything1
@quailpublishing

Follow the Junior Colour Knits blog at:
www.juniorcolourknits.co.uk

The Erika Knight yarn collection is distributed by Thomas B Ramsden. For further information please see **www.tbramsden.co.uk**